World War I

Scottish Tales of Adventure

Allan Burnett

BIRLINN

In memory of
Andrew Sinclair, John Sinclair and Frederick John Burnett –
Royal Scots

940.409411

First published in 2014 by
Birlinn Limited
West Newington House
10 Newington Road
Edinburgh
EH9 1QS

www.birlinn.co.uk

ISBN: 978 1 84158 932 9

British Library Cataloguing-in-Publication Data
A catalogue record for this book is available from the British Library

Typeset by Iolaire Typesetting, Newtonmore
Printed and bound by Grafica Veneta
www.graficaveneta.com

Contents

Introduction

Merry it was to laugh there –
Where death becomes absurd and life absurder.
For power was on us as we slashed bones bare
Not to feel sickness or remorse of murder.
Wilfred Owen

'Lads, you're wanted! Over there,'
Shiver in the morning dew,
More poor devils like yourselves
Waiting to be killed by you.
Ewart Alan Mackintosh

In this book of stories from the First World War, soldiers dodge snipers' bullets and hurl grenades at the unseen enemy while experimental breathing apparatus shields them from deadly gas.

Men piloting an amazing new invention called the aeroplane zoom through the clouds with guns blazing at their opponents.

Pioneering women doctors and their staff save soldiers' lives while they are bombarded with cannon-fire and chased through foreign lands.

They are stories of adventure and excitement, of courage and optimism. They are tales of triumph in adversity.

But the First World War was also about death and destruction on a gigantic scale, of intolerable misery and cruelty, often with no way out and no happy endings.

For me, these two sides to the war – the exhilarating and the miserable – are equally important. We need both to make sense of it, to comprehend why people went to fight in the first place, and to understand why there was so much regret after it was all over.

That is why the stories in this book also show aspects of the war's dark side. They demonstrate, too, how a soldier's fortunes often depended on luck.

Some people believe that luck is just down to chance, like rolling a dice. But others believe it is down to destiny or fate.

Take the moment that led to the outbreak of the First World War. It took place on a street corner in a city called Sarajevo, the capital of what was then Bosnia.

Back in the summer of 1914 a teenager called Gavrilo Princip stood there and pulled out a pistol. He took aim and shot dead a man called Archduke Franz Ferdinand and his wife Sophie, who were being driven past in their open-topped motor car.

The Archduke had been a very important person, and his friends swore revenge on Princip and his friends. One thing led to another, and eventually whole empires took sides over the issue, like gangs fighting in a playground – just on a far, far bigger scale.

On Princip's side were the Allies – the Russian, French and British empires, of which Scotland was part. And on the other side were the empires of Austro-Hungary, Turkey and Germany.

The result was the First World War.

When I was twelve years old, I stood in the exact spot where Gavrilo Princip had fired his gun more than three-quarters of a century earlier. I felt as though the assassin was still there, standing right next to me, and taking aim at his victims.

What would have happened, I wondered, if by chance the bullets had not hit their target? In fact, the Archduke was supposed to have been travelling by a different route for his own safety, but his driver took a wrong turn. If only the driver had not made that fateful error and given Princip his chance. The chain of events that followed might have been avoided.

Yet, perhaps the world was simply destined to go to war. The big empires were looking for an excuse to fight, and now they had it.

My experience in Sarajevo led me to think about other important questions too. Like, what did the First World War have to do with me? In time, I found some interesting answers.

I visited another city called Ypres in Belgium. You will read about what happened there in this book.

Some of the biggest and bloodiest battles of the First World War were fought around Ypres. The place was flattened and had to be rebuilt. A huge number of Scottish soldiers died there. In fact some historians conservatively estimate that over 100,000 Scots lost their lives in the First World War. Others argue that Scotland lost more men per head of population than any other country except Turkey and Serbia.

What's more, I learned that at least two of my own

great-grandfathers – and a great-great grandfather – had all fought in that war in a regiment called the Royal Scots.

One of them was sent to fight in a place called Gallipoli, in Turkey. One day, the battle trench he was in was hit by a bomb and it collapsed on top of him. Eventually his wiggling fingers could be seen protruding from the rubble and he was pulled out alive. Many of his friends were not so lucky.

These discoveries brought the war much closer to home.

Eventually I realised that the First World War had everything to do with my life, and with Scotland, the country I grew up in.

Every street, farm and island has its share of amazing and sorrowful First World War stories to tell. Chiselled into stone memorials in cities, towns and villages across the country are the names of the men who died.

The world they left behind was changed for ever.

The war brought new technology and new ways of doing things, as well as great anger about the loss of life. The people of Scotland were deeply affected.

While researching this book I discovered that the place I went for my daily walk was affected in its own special way, and seems to be haunted by some of the war's most famous figures. It is a hill with two summits that overlooks Edinburgh, the nation's capital, from the south-west. The hill, known as Craiglockhart, is adorned by woods, a golf course and some grand Victorian buildings.

Craiglockhart Hill gives a fine view of Edinburgh, where, during the First World War, huge cigar-shaped German airships hung in the sky next to the castle and dropped their bombs.

Edinburgh was the home town of Field Marshall Douglas Haig, commander of the British forces on the war's Western Front. Many historians believe the Allied victory that ended the

First World War in 1918 was largely thanks to Haig's determined leadership, his inspirational battle tactics and his ability to rally the troops.

At least, that is one side of the story.

The other way of looking at it is that Haig, and other war leaders, made errors that doomed hundreds of thousands of men to a miserable death.

That was the opinion of one wounded English officer who looked out over Edinburgh from Craiglockhart Hill in the autumn of 1917. His name was Wilfred Owen. He was a patient at Craiglockhart War Hospital, a building that still stands on the hill today.

Owen was treated for an illness called 'shell shock', which was caused by the stress of intense combat in the trenches. During his treatment at the hospital Owen played golf, taught at a local school, and became friends with another patient called Siegfried Sassoon.

Sassoon wrote poetry to express his feelings about the war. He encouraged Owen to do the same. Eventually Owen was returned to duty, but he was killed in battle in November 1918, just a few days before the war ended.

Another powerful poet who was killed in action during the war was Ewart Alan Mackintosh. He was a Gaelic-speaker and bagpipe player whose family came from the Highlands. His Scottish regiment, the Seaforth Highlanders, was led proudly into battle by pipes and drums only for its young recruits to be smashed and broken in their hundreds by bombs and bullets.

The words of Mackintosh and Owen – some of which appear at the beginning of this Introduction – continue to live and grow long after the poets' lives were cut short. Their poetry emphasises the barbarity and hopelessness of the First World War. But even so, it is beautiful.

By showing us the worst of what human beings are capable of, it makes us try harder to bring out the best.

The Teacher Threw a Bomb

At around 9.30pm torchlights appeared at the far end of the street, accompanied by music and marching boots. 'The soldiers are coming!' shouted a boy perched high up on a glowing street lamp.

The crowd's pent-up excitement exploded. They clapped, cheered, roared and whistled. Flags and handkerchiefs waved from tenement windows above. The grand farewell had begun.

First came the band. Bagpipes blared. Kilts flared in the breeze. Tubas and trombones blasted. Bass drums boomed and snares rat-a-tat-tatted.

Then followed the rest of the men, in rows four abreast, some singing songs of war as their trrrump-trrrump-trrrump bootsteps echoed off the grey granite walls. The bonnets on their heads swam along in formation like a shoal of exotic fish from the great North Sea.

Now and then, a young woman broke through the crowd barrier and rushed forward. She would throw her arms around a soldier's neck and kiss him, only to be hurled away by a hard-hearted sergeant. The memory of the bristle of her sweetheart's moustache on her cheek and whisky breath from his last drink at his home barracks was her prize.

George Ramage was not expecting female attention, but he got it anyway. Marching on the edge of the procession, he found himself being handed presents from unknown women. He was already carrying a heavy backpack, a rifle and 120 rounds of ammunition – but since the presents were mostly cigarettes they were a welcome additional burden. Fags, he had heard, could be bartered for other goodies once they reached the front line.

Ramage was thirty-three years old. Before joining the army, he had been a teacher down in Edinburgh. Some of the lads marching with him were almost young enough to be his pupils.

The soldiers completed their march from King Street Barracks to the station next to Union Square. The waiting locomotive impatiently belched out smoke and steam as men piled into the carriages. Ramage hauled himself aboard. The guard blew his whistle and the doors began to slam.

By 10pm the train was crawling out of Aberdeen and soon the wheels were clickety-clacking over the rail joints, as darkened fields sped past. Ramage saw himself and the others reflected in the carriage's ink-black windows. There were eighty-five men in his draft – off to join the 1st Battalion, Gordon Highlanders, as part of the British Expeditionary Force in France and Belgium. Some were excited first-time recruits, but others were wounded and unsmiling veterans returning to the firing line.

The veterans had been promised that the war – declared on 4 August 1914 – would be over by Christmas. Well, Christmas had been and gone and the German Empire, which had advanced across Europe, remained undefeated.

Ramage was one of those who had enlisted early in the new year, on 19 January 1915. He was ordered to Aberdeen, where his battalion was based, for training in preparation for deployment. It was now 13 April and his wartime adventure was about to begin.

By noon the next day the train had crossed the Scottish border and was well into England. They arrived at Southampton docks at a quarter to four. The steamer was waiting. Up the gangway went Ramage and company, joining other drafts for the infantry, cavalry and engineers.

Ramage found a space on deck to sleep and the next morning woke to witness the vessel entering the mouth of the River Seine, having safely crossed the English Channel to France. Dozens of other steamers were sailing about alongside torpedo boats and minesweeping trawlers.

On the bank of the river stood the port city of Le Havre – its name French for 'The Harbour'. Near the water's edge was a hoarding that read 'God Bless You All'. A French soldier dressed in a blue coat and baggy red trousers waved a salute.

Further on, more well-wishers flocked to the banks. Behind them lay fields, beyond which were white cliffs with pretty chateaux perched on top. School bells rang out, rifles fired in the air and dogs barked in greeting. 'Heep Heep Hooray!' shouted a group of women, waving handkerchiefs and flags, their feet soaked by the wash as the troopship sped past. Ramage couldn't help waving back.

At lunchtime the vessel reached its destination, the city of Rouen. As the soldiers marched uphill to spend the night in a British camp, Ramage noticed that many of the locals here seemed gloomier, although some of the women perked up when they noticed the Scotsmen's kilts and bare legs.

The final stage of Ramage's journey to the front was by train. Tightly packed in a cushionless carriage, and with lumps in their throats, the men began to sing songs they'd learned at school. 'Me and my true love will never meet again, on the bonnie bonnie banks of Loch Lomond . . .'

To avoid becoming too homesick, they followed that with an upbeat ragtime jazz song, 'We are the Gordon swells boys, we are the Gordon swells!'

In the morning they made a few stops. Some were brief, just long enough for locals to pass bottles of wine through the carriage windows in exchange for tins of 'bully beef' – a type of tinned corned beef which was the mainstay of the soldiers' rations.

Other stops were longer. At Hazebrouck, a French town about ten miles from the Belgian border, Ramage washed under a water pipe used to fill the trains' steam engines. Then, while someone made tea, he and his friends watched transfixed as two military aeroplanes – still a dazzling new invention – shimmered in the sunshine overhead.

At last, just as the men were growing tired and argumentative from hours spent in the cramped carriage, the train made its final stop at Bailleul. They were now very close to the border with Belgium and the front line beyond. Bailleul's sleepy old streets, rudely awakened by war, were swarming with soldiers, horses and army motor vehicles. Ramage and the others marched through the town and began a six-mile hike north, to the billets – the place where they would sleep until sent to the trenches.

They rested en route in a ploughed field. It was here, while lying on the freshly turned soil, that Ramage heard the distant sound of man-made thunder for the first time. He jerked his head up to listen.

BOOM ... BOOM ... BOOM ... The guns of war. Suddenly the thought struck him that he might never see home again.

The billets were a welcome sight, wooden huts with corrugated-iron roofs sloping down to the ground. The soldiers had crossed the border into Belgium a couple of miles back and were now in a place called La Clytte. The British field guns – huge, long-barrelled cannons – were located nearby. Every time they fired, the huts shook.

About four miles further on to the north-east was the city of Ypres – pronounced 'Eee-prey' – a major battle zone. The Gordon Highlanders were part of a line defending the land around Ypres. Their goal was to stop the Germans advancing west to the coast, beyond Ypres, and capturing the French port of Calais.

At night, while searchlight beams hunted for aircraft overhead, the giant field guns fired time after time on the enemy trenches. With each strike, broad flashes lit up the sky. To Ramage, it looked as if the door of an immense iron furnace was being opened and shut. The flashes were accompanied by loud booms, like breakers hitting sea cliffs. The distant rifle and machine-gun fire echoed like rivets being hammered into a ship's hull.

By day, elderly local farm workers sowed seeds on the edge of the battlefield with gnarled hands, wiping sweat off their wrinkled faces as they went. Their home was a war zone, yet they tried to continue as if nothing had happened.

Ramage was kept busy by being drilled, marched and inspected. The reality of what he had signed up for was becoming clearer as each day passed, and never more so than when he listened while an officer read out cases in which the death sentence had been passed on Tommies – the nickname for British soldiers – for disobeying orders.

This was no idle threat. One man had refused to go to the trenches with his platoon. So he was put in front of a firing squad and shot. Another deserted his post in the trenches – he too was shot. An officer in the firing line took cover without permission and for this he was also shot.

At last it was time for Ramage's first stint in the battle trenches. At 7pm on Thursday, 22 April 1915, he and the rest of the men of No 16 Platoon, D Company, 1st Gordons, cleaned their huts and departed, carrying all their possessions in their backpacks and pouches. These included two days' rations of bully beef, biscuits, bread, cheese, sugar and tea. Not forgetting their 'smokes' – another Tommy word for cigarettes.

No halting. No speaking. No smoking. These were the orders as the men marched along in the gathering darkness, stray bullets whizzing past their ears. They passed ruined farmsteads and the remains of shattered trenches, and skirted round the edges of huge craters left by exploding bombshells.

A bombshell – or 'shell', as they called them – typically contained a high-explosive that threw out hot chunks of jagged metal, called shrapnel, on impact. Walking past numerous roughly marked soldiers' graves, Ramage was in no doubt about the shells' destructive powers.

The artillery used in the First World War was the most powerful the world had seen. But nobody had yet devised a method for men to advance against such firepower without being slaughtered. So each side spent most of their time hiding in trenches to stay alive.

A star shell flared up just ahead. These shells were designed not to destroy, but to illuminate. The field was turned a vivid green. Objects stood out as though under a bright electric light. Ramage and the others crouched down, motionless. When the flare died down, they slipped silently into their portion of the trench just as the company they were relieving slipped out.

'Fix bayonets!' someone shouted.

Just as they'd been trained to do, the men attached blades to the ends of their Lee Enfield rifles – ready to skewer a German should one jump into the trench unexpectedly. The German trench was only sixty metres away – about the width of a football pitch – in front of some woods.

Even closer to the Germans were men of the Royal Scots regiment. Their trenches were only thirty metres apart. The short stretch of ground in between – the length of a swimming pool – was referred to as No Man's Land.

Ramage looked around at his new accommodation. The trench was not actually dug into the ground as trenches usually were. It was mostly above ground, and more like a rampart – two walls made of piled-up sandbags filled with heavy clayey soil, with a channel or 'trench' in between. Inside the trench was a long bench for sitting on, or standing to watch German movements.

'We've been stuck in the same spot for months,' said a war-weary Tommy to Ramage as he packed up to go. 'I've never seen a German yet and never fired a shot.'

In fact, Ramage's section of the trench didn't shoot, for they would hit the Royal Scots if they did. Everyone else along the front seemed to fire bullets and bombs all night long. But neither side advanced an inch.

Night fell and rats scurried over resting bodies as the hours crawled by. Eventually the dawn began to break. The men took turns to keep watch using periscopes – long, tube-like devices containing mirrors and lenses that allowed the user to peep over the parapet while remaining hidden.

When Ramage looked out, he noted three rows of 'knife-rests' – barbed-wire defences designed to entangle an advancing enemy and make him easy prey for British machine guns. Ramage also saw that any building not already flattened was a ruin, and that the bark of all the trees had been shredded by bullets and shrapnel.

A few metres in front of the trench a dead soldier lay on his back. His bloated corpse had apparently lain there since December. Nobody dared retrieve him or they would simply have been added to the body count.

Behind the trench were graves marked by crosses. The clayey soil around them was strewn with disused sandbags, empty food tins and other rubbish.

'Anyone got a wristwatch? Swap you anything you like,' said one Tommy.

'I see you've got a few packs of fags,' replied another. 'Give me the lot and my watch is yours.'

Apart from trading belongings or being on watch duty, pastimes included cooking, cleaning and searching for lice. An infestation of the tiny parasites was enough to drive a man mad scratching himself to pieces. Ramage thanked God he didn't have any – yet.

Relief from this hellish existence was a cup of tea. That is, if a tepid brew made from scummy, vermin-infested bubbling green water scooped from shell holes could be called 'tea'. Ramage, like many inexperienced Tommies, had drunk the clean water in his canteen too quickly. His rations were running out pretty quickly too.

Further relief came from letting off a few rounds of fire against the enemy. Ramage would poke his rifle through a 'keyhole' – a firing hole cut in an iron shield mounted on the sandbag parapet – and shoot at the Germans.

Days and nights passed. It began to rain and the clay turned to mud. Every remaining piece of unsoiled kit or uniform became dirty. All Ramage could do was to drag a waterproof sheet around his shoulders and wait for the rain to stop.

An empty ration tin filled with some kind of chemical liquid was hung up on a post along with a bag of cloth scraps. This was in case of a gas attack. If poisonous clouds were spotted blowing in their direction, the sentries would soak the cloths and give one to each man to put over his face.

The Germans must have been just as frustrated. Their snipers' bullets smashed the ends of the British periscopes and their shells whistled overhead. Every now and then one would land nearby, perhaps thirty metres off, tearing up the ground.

Neither side let up. But neither side made any real progress.

On his last night in the trench, Ramage was told he was going to become a grenadier – a bomb-thrower.

It felt good to have been chosen for the job. It was well known that trainee grenadiers were selected from men who were the best, bravest and steadiest in an emergency. He must have done well so far. A grenadier could do a lot of damage if he hit the target.

Plus, the training meant he would not have to return to his company's trenches for a while.

'It's not as cushy as it sounds,' said one Tommy, as Ramage passed him. 'Two days ago there were three casualties among the bomb-throwers in this battalion. And that was just when they were practising.'

During his training, Ramage was shown the grave of the

grenadier whose place he was taking. The poor chap had accidentally blown himself up. Determined not to let that happen to him, Ramage worked hard to learn the skills of a grenadier, which included using catapults and trench mortars, the small mobile cannons that made a 'plop!' sound when their stumpy, upturned barrels were fired.

After a couple more days of training, Ramage and his colleagues were ordered into battle. At 10pm, under a golden moon, they wheeled barrows of mortars, bombs and grenades to the nearby village of Kemmel. As quietly as they could, they wove their way around shell craters and through ruined streets until they reached a communication trench – a waterlogged, muddy channel that led to the trench in which they'd be based that night. Once they had finished hauling the weapons into position they got to work.

PLOP! The first mortar fired.

BOOM! It hit the German side.

Six more bombs were launched beautifully before the Germans replied with a grenade that exploded five metres away from Ramage, showering him in soil. Luckily for him it was on the other side of a protective wall called a traverse.

But those on the other side of the traverse were not so lucky. They had been resting, chatting or cooking when the German bomb exploded. When the smoke cleared, Ramage peeked over the traverse. Four men were wounded – two seriously in the stomach, arms, head and feet. There was a lot of blood.

'Pass word for stretcher bearers!' somebody called in the darkness.

'Ramage, get your eyes off the wounded and return to your mortar!' the bombing officer commanded.

It was hard to concentrate. One of the wounded, a veteran,

died hours later. As Ramage trudged back through the mist at dawn, his first night's bombing over, he couldn't help reflecting on the wastefulness and stupidity of war.

News arrived that made it clear Ramage could be using his new skills again very soon. The battalion was being redeployed as a reserve for trenches expected to suffer high casualties. They had to be ready to move out at a moment's notice.

In the meantime they received an unexpected 'treat' – a bath. Having recently discovered lice on his own body, Ramage eagerly climbed in – even if the tub had to be shared with another man, in water that had already been used by other filthy Tommies. It was thick with milky disinfectant and slime.

The bath was followed by a rub down with a towel, and a clean shirt. Ramage tried to ignore the dead lice stuck to it. 'Oh I love Aberdeen and I love my Queen,' he sang along with the other soldiers, trying to keep his spirits up. They were all glad of the wash and change of clothes, but dreading what was coming next.

A few miles away, Ypres was being bombarded. As night fell a bright yellow glow showed where German incendiary bombs were setting buildings on fire. The sky was red and clouds of smoke enveloped the city's towers and spires, including those of Cloth Hall – a huge medieval market where merchants had bought and sold wool for centuries.

Ramage joined a huddle of soldiers sitting around a brazier – an upright metal box containing a coal fire. The firelight shone through holes in the brazier's sides, giving the men's faces a ruddy glow. Meanwhile, beyond the nearby woods and fields, the people of Ypres ran in terror from their burning homes.

Early the next morning a magnificent-looking general on horseback addressed them all. 'Men, you are about to go to one of the most dangerous places in the war. A place where an entire brigade has been decimated. A place where the trenches have been smashed flat. A place where the enemy has unleashed gas . . .'

'Perhaps he wants us to start digging our own graves right now,' muttered one old soldier.

'And yet,' the general continued, 'it is also a place where the spirit of the men has not been broken. You Gordons are a very distinguished regiment with a great history. You are Scots, and I am perfectly certain you will never retreat . . .!'

'Same old bloody muck,' muttered another war-weary veteran.

At lunchtime they set off towards their destination close to Hill 60 – a strategically advantageous bit of raised ground. They passed motor vehicles carrying anti-aircraft guns. Then a row of gigantic field guns. They marched through a village where children played in the warm sunshine as shells whooshed overhead with a sound like roaring crowds. It was an unsettling sight.

They passed within a mile of Ypres. Smoke from the fires hung in the air. Then they made their way along a railway track lined with shattered telegraph poles and broken wires. Dugouts were cut into the embankment below the track, forming shelters for the men and First Aid posts – known as 'dressing stations' – for the wounded. Stretcher-bearers hurried in and out.

The trench near Hill 60 was cold and wet. Ramage regretted his earlier decision to abandon his cardigan, jacket and spare socks to save weight. As he settled in with the other men, he tried to console himself with the thought that the Germans on the other side of No Man's Land were being pounded to Hell by the British gunners. The shells flew in low over the British trench. Ramage and the others ducked instinctively. Shrapnel showered on impact, German sandbags went flying. This would not be a quick job.

A couple of days later while fetching water, Ramage came across abandoned enemy trenches and saw German soldiers for the first time. All three were dead. One had been shot through the forehead. Another had had the top of his head blown off by a shell. The third was lying on his face in a pool of blood.

Death had turned their hands to wax, their faces yellow and blueish. The corpses had been robbed, their valuable buttons cut off. Broken equipment, bent rifles, rusty ammunition and unexploded bombs lay all around.

That night Ramage slept badly – his mind replaying the day's images as he wriggled about in his shirt, trying to keep warm.

The next day dawned sunny and warm, and Ramage's company was ordered up to the firing line. The men were surprised by the order. Wasn't this the firing line? The enemy was only a hundred metres away and there was plenty of firing going on. But their orders were clear. They had to get closer.

While waiting for the command to move, they brewed tea and made hot bully beef. A German sniper must have spotted the smoke from their tiny fire and let loose a shot. His bullet burst a sandbag in the parapet, sending a shower of dry clay down into their tea. But they still drank it. Not long afterwards the word came that they were to set off.

Eventually, after dark, they reached their new destination. The thunder of shells made Ramage's ears ring. This trench was massive, dug into the ground with a high parapet of neatly piled sandbags to protect it. He climbed into a coffin-shaped dugout hoping for some rest but was soon called back out to join a bomb-throwing party in another section of the trench.

The Germans were now fewer than forty metres away. The danger was intense. One man was shot through the heart while trying to position a knife-rest in the dark; another looked over the parapet for the briefest of seconds and had his brains blown out.

This section of trench and the land around it was like a cross between a rubbish heap, a sewer and a graveyard. Discarded tins and rusty equipment lay in slimy soil, heaving with corpses, some of which were sprinkled with chloride of lime to stop them rotting and smelling.

The weather took a turn for the worse, and as the rain beat down Ramage watched men wrap themselves in waterproof sheets before stuffing their bodies into muddy, stinking dugouts. He was ejected from his own dugout by an officer who wanted it for himself, and had to dig another. At least the physical activity took his mind off the danger.

But any prospect of rest was soon shattered by new orders. Ramage was assigned to a listening post and given command of a group of sentries. Listening posts protruded from the front line like tentacles reaching toward the German trenches. They had to be close if the British soldiers were to be able to spy on the enemy.

Ramage was only a few metres away from the enemy now, close enough to hear the chatter of German voices. He and his sentries had to remain as silent as possible. One wrong move or sound and a man would quickly get a bullet or bayonet in his belly.

After peering into the night air for two hours Ramage saw two dark objects appearing out of the gloom. 'Germans!' he whispered to himself.

He slowly curled his finger round the trigger of his rifle, his eyes fixed. 'They moved!' he told himself. 'They're going to shoot at me!' His palms were slick with sweat, his mouth dry. He got ready to open fire.

Suddenly, a star shell lit up the ground, revealing that the two objects were just sandbags. Ramage let out a sigh, his nerves in shreds.

At midnight Ramage received orders from the captain. 'Send man up comm trench to search for two of mine. They got lost in skirmish with enemy.'

Ramage immediately found a volunteer, who quickly returned. He had rescued the missing men, and found a body too. When Ramage relayed this information to his captain, he was ordered to take his volunteer and go back himself to see if the body was one of their own.

Ramage found the body – a swollen, six-foot giant with its face crushed down in the mud. Crouching down, he looked to see if the man was wearing a kilt or not. A star shell burst above him and he saw it was a trousered officer, not a Gordon. Not one of their own. He reported back.

Soon he was ordered further up the trench on a new search – this time for a wounded Gordon. Leaving his rifle to make movement easier, he cautiously entered a German communication trench.

Suddenly there was a blaze of rifle fire ten or fifteen metres in front of him. Ramage froze. 'Please don't shoot me in the face!' he prayed silently, screwing up his eyes.

When he opened them and found he was still standing, he quickly threw himself against the trench wall and crouched down before the next star shell lit him up like a sitting duck.

Just then, another star shell burst and Ramage saw a kilted soldier moving behind a small parapet next to the trench he was in. He crept up to within just three metres of the parapet, terrified of being shot by friend or foe.

'Gordon!' he whispered hoarsely to identify himself. 'Any wounded?'

'None!' came the hushed reply.

Ramage turned to make his way back through the pitch black and came within seconds of being shot by his own sentries. But there was no time to rest. He was ordered to take a couple of stretcher bearers and go and retrieve the body of the trousered officer. When they reached it, they found that his head had been blown off and that the body was too decayed to be removed. They had no choice but to leave the officer in his open grave.

The next day was warm. The stench of death hung in the air. Ramage got half a cup of water to wash in, but his aching limbs and soapy hands lost their grip and he dropped the cup onto the duckboards at the bottom of the trench. He was utterly exhausted.

In the early hours of the following morning, after a night's heavy bombardment, the men were relieved from the front line and marched thirteen excruciating miles back to La Clytte. Ramage had never been more grateful for a fresh cup of tea, which he drank while he opened parcels he had received from Scotland containing oranges and mince pies. It was 6am before he collapsed in sleep.

He awoke feeling like an old, worn-out cart horse – aching all over. During the next few days the men drilled or rested. They smoked, read, played dominoes and sometimes argued. Hymns were sung to lift spirits. But the respite never lasted long. Without any warning, they would be ordered to march.

By evening the following day they were in Ypres. The fire-bombing Ramage had witnessed had done its job. Every building was either damaged or incinerated. The cathedral and Cloth Hall were in ruins. Curtains flapped from the shattered windows of bombed-out homes. Floorboards in the upper storey of an apartment hung in the air, the outer wall of the building now blasted away. Furniture teetered on the edge of the chasm.

Music wafted eerily across the rubble. A crackling gramophone player had been set up at the entrance to a bombed-out café where exhausted Tommies sat listening. When Ramage peeped through a shuttered ground-floor window, he could see a group of cheerful officers sitting round a table topped with lots of good food and a whisky bottle. All right for some.

With nearby shellfire occasionally shaking the ground, the men continued, crossing a canal bridge and trudging along a filthy railway cutting. They passed two dead Tommies with rain-flecked sheets where their heads used to be. Ramage couldn't help becoming angry as he thought about the officers drinking and feasting in their cosy little den while these men lay abandoned and unburied.

Once beyond the cutting, they were ordered to dig new trenches.

When Ramage lay down the next day, cold, exhausted and hungry, he dreamed of having a hot clean bath, fresh comfortable clothes, and gorging on fish-and-chips and lemonade before sleeping like a cat. That night, after a long struggle, he made his own dugout, only for two sergeants to appear and claim it for themselves.

'Thieves!' he growled, but they ignored him. Ramage was infuriated by their selfishness.

The next couple of days passed uneventfully except for the riot of lice chomping Ramage's skin and the relentless hunger pangs in his belly. A day's rations were barely enough to survive on, let alone tackle the physical work they being ordered to do. An inch of cheese, six biscuits, a small tin of bully beef, a tin of jam to be shared among seven men, and sometimes a tiny piece of ham no bigger than a penny.

While deepening one of the communication trenches, Ramage felt so weak he could hardly push the spade into the soil. When he found a sod of turf with a small turnip sprouting from it, he was so hungry that he tried to eat it, but it was as tough, dry and wizened as cork. Thank God they were eventually allowed to make a fire and brew some tea.

It was almost the end of May. Ramage and his company were moved once more to the front-line trenches, near a railway embankment. Things were eerily quiet but no less dangerous.

While resting on a board in his trench, Ramage savoured a Turkish cigarette. Suddenly he heard the crack of a bullet at his ear, then another striking the earth in front of him. A sniper must have seen the wisp of smoke. 'Damn him!' cursed Ramage, hurriedly stubbing out his fag. 'I was enjoying that.'

June began with a terrific bombardment. Ramage had never experienced anything like it. Whopping German shells slammed into the ground and burst, releasing hot, jagged chunks of shrapnel in every direction. Branches were torn from trees and flung through the air. Smoke billowed amid flames as men dived for cover. It wasn't long before Ramage's ear drums were close to bursting.

'This is the worst since the 1st Gordons were annihilated in the Battle of the Marne last year,' muttered one veteran.

'Keep your bloody heads down!' cried another.

'How much longer will I survive this?' wondered Ramage.

He was crouching between the embankment and a hedge when a hunk of hot iron shrapnel the size of a golf ball hit his leg.

Mercifully it had first passed through the hedge, which slowed it down to a relatively harmless velocity.

After three days of relentless German firepower, Ramage was intensely glad when his platoon was relieved and withdrawn to dugouts behind the lines. Yet the random barbarity continued. A brave, hard-working soldier was shot in the neck after joking about how good it would be to get 'a cushy one' – a wound that was not fatal but still serious enough to get you sent home. Another was shot and killed right next to Ramage as they drew water from a well.

The days dragged on. After another brief stint in a trench at the firing-line, Ramage and his platoon were sent to a rest camp. They marched through the outskirts of Ypres then got a lift on a motor bus. The camp was neither restful nor comfortable, and they slept in an open field wrapped in waterproof sheets.

But there were compensations. A mug of beer, payment of ten francs and a letter from home cheered Ramage up. He even found a little sign written by a soldier and placed in a field next to a cluster of chicks: 'Be careful, bird's nest'.

Otherwise the men entertained themselves with football, concerts and pillow fights. But they all knew that they would be back on the front line before very long.

Eventually Ramage's platoon was ordered back into action. With shovels resting on their shoulders, they marched through a village where the church had been so recently burned out that its floorboards were still glowing. They passed a dead horse lying by the side of the road.

They marched back into Ypres and Ramage got a closer look at the damage to Cloth Hall. The central tower was wrecked, its clock stopped at 5.25. Statues still stood in niches around the outer wall, reminding him of Scotland's national museum in Edinburgh.

As they continued to make their way through the town Ramage noticed a rusting metal safe at the side of the road. Its door was open and papers were scattered all around. No doubt looters had taken anything of value.

Eventually, they reached their destination – a spot where they had orders to dig a trench to lay communication wires. It was hard going, but they set to work, and once the job was done they got a lift back to the rest camp in the middle of the night. However, their stay there was brief.

The next evening they were sent into Ypres yet again and billeted in a store which they were to guard. Ramage was made corporal of the guard and watched as his sentries returned from looting sprees, bringing with them tins of jam and salmon, and sour wine.

A one-armed Frenchman was brought before Ramage for interrogation after he was found apparently looting a house. However, he produced the papers to prove he was removing things on the orders of the house-owner so Ramage set him free with his wagonload of furniture. Even if he is looting, thought Ramage, who are we to judge?

Ramage decided that it was unlikely there would be trouble in Ypres that night. He had taken his shirt off to check for lice and was sitting in the store writing a letter when the sergeant major arrived unannounced.

'Get your shirt on, Ramage! It's time to do some real work. There's going to be an advance and you are needed for bomb-throwing duties.'

At last, thought Ramage – a chance for a proper fight instead of hiding in the trenches. He was marched to a dilapidated barracks with the coats of arms of Belgian towns painted on the walls. Here he was kitted out with new equipment and ammunition.

Ramage and company were sent to occupy some captured German trenches. They were to stay there and await the order to go over the top and run at the enemy with their grenades.

'Poison gas ahead!' said one wounded Tommy, as he passed them in the other direction.

Immediately the order went out. They were to put on their protective equipment. Each soldier had been issued with a 'smoke helmet' – a cloth bag he pulled over his head and tucked into his collar, with a clear-plastic panel to see through.

The smoke helmet made the going much harder. It left the soldiers looking like primitive spacemen from one of the science-fiction novels that were so popular at the time, stumbling through an alien world as they hauled their grenades along a dark, shell-blasted communication trench. Ramage was at the rear and could hardly see where he was going. Several times he stumbled and began giggling inside his cloth helmet at the ridiculousness of it all.

Finally, fed up with not being able to see properly, he tore off his helmet. Instantly he got a whiff off something that was like petrol mixed with garlic. His eyes began to burn and well up. Realising his mistake, he pulled on the helmet again and kept plodding along.

Some of the soldiers didn't act as quickly, so the men at the front halted to wait for those who had fallen behind. Several men vomited because of the gas. One was shot dead. Another was blown up by a shell. Eventually the remaining soldiers received further orders.

'Bombers this way!' shouted an officer.

Ramage and his colleagues followed, shells bursting all around.

The protective cloak of darkness was beginning to give way to early light.

They carried on along another trench, stepping past broken bodies, until they reached the captured German trenches. First the corpses of British soldiers had to be moved. One dead Tommy was in a crouching position with his hands over his face. Another was twisted into a recess in the trench wall. Bloated and frozen with rigor mortis they were difficult to shift, and Ramage's camouflaged khaki kilt apron was soon as bloody as that of a butcher's.

Ramage was then ordered to go with some men to guard a forward communication trench linking the captured trenches with those still under German control. Moving stealthily, his head ducked, he arrived to find the trench full of more dead bodies. Most had horrifying wounds, and they were piled up in heaps – Tommies on top of Germans. It was difficult to know where to start.

'They've done me in this time.'

Ramage spun round, surprised to hear signs of life. It was a severely wounded soldier with four good-conduct and long service stripes on his sleeve, lying on a waterproof sheet with another sheet blanketing him. Next to him was a boy, no more than sixteen years old, with a broken leg. He jabbered in agony when Ramage and the others, ignorant of first aid, tried their best to tend to him. Ramage put some water to the boy's lips, and then to those of the old soldier.

As morning crept in, the bombing corporal made tea for the wounded while Ramage comforted another casualty whose wounds had not been dressed. A handsome fellow of about thirty-five, he turned his tired face to Ramage and said, 'Help me to sit up, would you?'

As Ramage did so he discovered the flesh on the man's back was all bloody. Ramage called for a stretcher and began binding the man's wounds. 'Damn the inhumanity of war!' he cursed.

News came that the attack in which Ramage was to take part had been abandoned. He greeted this with frustration. In spite of everything, he was bursting to get at the enemy.

He almost cried with excitement, therefore, when he saw a group of Germans moving in the dawn light. Their spiked helmets were about 250 metres away as they worked to repair a battered trench, their shovels tossing earth in the air.

Ramage had a clear shot. Through gas-fuddled eyes he aimed his rifle and fired, but it seemed to have little effect. Even when a German officer turned his back to him Ramage still couldn't hit the target.

'Germans are coming!' somebody barked. 'We need three good shots to snipe at them!'

Still itching to do what he had been trained for, Ramage ordered two privates to follow him, which they did reluctantly, and he headed up the trench to cut off the advancing enemy.

Ramage took up position, leaning on a corner. He set his rifle and began sniping. To get a better rest for his elbows, he found himself standing on the back of a dead Tommy whose body squelched in the mud – still doing his bit, even in death.

For an hour Ramage shot at the Germans, with what effect he did not know. Eventually, when it appeared the enemy had withdrawn, he was pulled back.

Sent to another trench with a jacket full of grenades, Ramage was given new orders to take command of eight grenadiers and set up two new bombing posts. During the watches the men were to keep their eyes peeled for any advancing Germans, bombs at the ready.

By 7am, Ramage was in desperate need of a rest. He stood up to throw his waterproof sheet over his shoulders. It was all the enemy sniper required. From around sixty metres away a German soldier pulled the trigger on a Mauser Gewehr 98 rifle. The bullet exploded from the barrel and flew through the air at almost 1,000 metres per second, in the direction of Ramage's forehead.

CRACK!

Ramage screamed. His vision blanked, his brain went fuzzy. He was aware of blood pouring from his body.

'My hand . . .' he gasped.

The bullet had struck his left hand, which had been just a few centimetres away from his face, severing two fingers and making a hole in his palm.

Ramage sank to his knees, clutching his shattered hand at the wrist. An officer calmed him and began bandaging the wound, and he lost consciousness for a while. His sleep might have been permanent if the Mauser had not been notoriously inaccurate at short range.

Before Ramage could be sent back to the dressing station, darkness had to fall. While they waited, his comrades showed great compassion: laying him down gently, lighting his cigarettes, making him tea, and sharing their rations. As he prepared to leave he shared out his belongings with them, including his rifle, which he knew he would no longer need.

Ramage's combat service was ended by a single bullet in Hooge, outside Ypres, on 18 June 1915. There would be no more forced marches, no more rifle inspections, no shortage of food, no hard cold beds or sleepless nights, no muddy clothes, no shells or bullets, and no danger or excitement. Provided he made it to the dressing station alive.

This he did, and his hand was re-bandaged. He learned there that the wounded chap he had bandaged up two nights previously had died from exposure. Ramage was more fortunate. A doctor put him on an ambulance which took him into Ypres, where the wounded were being collected. Two stretcher cases lay next to him in the jiggling, swaying vehicle. Ramage couldn't ignore the death rattle from one of them – a gurgling sound that told everybody he would need no further treatment.

Ramage was forwarded to a hospital at Le Treport, on the French coast, where he was given a proper bath. His hand was seriously infected and more fingers had to be cut off. After a few days he was taken down the coast to Dieppe and put on a boat heading across the English Channel for Britain.

In a sanatorium in Hastings, on the south coast of England, Ramage was operated on to remove more bone from his hand. Eventually he became well enough to go out walking on the promenade along the seafront, dressed in a fresh kilt, with his arm in a sling.

In Hastings, Ramage was treated like a hero. Women he had never met lavished him with gifts, shopkeepers gave him matches and cigarettes for free, people made way for him wherever he went.

Eventually he was permitted to visit his family in Aberdeen. There he began to plan for the future. He attended classes in botany and zoology at the city's university. But soon he had to head back south to a hospital in Roehampton, London, where he was fitted with an artificial hand and, eventually, an artificial arm.

Ramage felt lucky. One of the other patients had been blinded in one eye and lost both hands. Before his artificial hands were fitted, the man wrote letters to his wife using pencils tied to his stumps. Two other handless men read newspapers by opening the pages with their teeth. Others hobbled about on artificial legs. 'It's impossible to tell the real from the artificial,' lied the staff. They meant well, of course, but the injured soldiers knew better.

When Ramage was discharged, he was given a new pair of boots, an overcoat and a railway pass – plus a little money to get him restarted in civilian life. He headed for the railway station and arrived back home in Scotland, where he received his army discharge papers, dated 30 August 1916.

George Ramage's war was finally over. He wrote in his diary:

Thus ends my active military experience . . . enjoyable on the whole, though the feeling of the utter stupidity of war was ever present. Why then did I join the army? Was it following the mob, in other words, cowardice?

For my own self esteem let me say that was not the reason. Here it is. War is a hellish travesty of humanity, yet as long as one nation is prepared by force of arms and by its consequent slaughter, disfigurement and devastation, to overthrow the liberties and destroy the lives of other nations, each nation must be prepared and ready to resist to the death.

WAR REPORT

Personnel: Lance Corporal George Ramage was born in Sunderland in April 1882, the son of a Scottish artisan metal-worker. Ramage was brought up in Aberdeen by two aunts and considered himself a Scotsman. He was educated at the city's university and after obtaining his degree, became a primary-school teacher in Ayrshire and Edinburgh.

In January 1915 Ramage enlisted with Aberdeenshire regiment, the Gordon Highlanders. That April he joined the 1st Battalion Gordons in the battlefields of northern France and Belgium, a region also known as Flanders. He worked as a grenadier – or bomb-thrower – in and around Ypres.

Badly wounded in the hand in June, he was taken to England for treatment and fitted with an artificial arm. After the war he returned to Edinburgh and taught at Sciennes Primary School. He took frequent holidays in Aberdeen and on the continent. In spite of his artificial hand he enjoyed playing the piano. He was well-liked by his pupils and died aged just 51 in March 1934.

Event Log: Ramage took part in the Allied defence of the Ypres salient. The Allies were British, French, Belgian and Canadian forces. The city of Ypres is in Belgium, on its border with France. A salient is an area of ground that projects from friendly territory into enemy territory, and therefore is almost completely surrounded by hostile forces.

The Allies' goal was to stop the German army advancing beyond Ypres and into north-western France. The British nicknamed Ypres 'Wipers' because most of them couldn't pronounce it properly.

Ypres was on the Western Front – a line of opposing trenches almost 500 miles long. It snaked from the Belgian coast all the way to Switzerland. Advancing from the front's north-east side was the German army, while on the south-west side were the British, French and other Allies.

By the time Ramage arrived at Ypres in 1915, the German advance had been halted by the Allies. Both sides had dug into protective trenches, but found they were barely able to move forward because the firepower on the other side was too great and the enemy defences too strong. The situation was a deadlock – neither side was able to defeat the other.

Ramage experienced the Second Battle of Ypres and its aftermath in May and June 1915. He witnessed the German bombardment of the city, which was part of their attempt to break through the Allied lines, and experienced smaller battles at Hooge and Bellewaarde on its fringes. The Germans took Hooge in May with the help of poison gas, but in June the Allies retook some of the lost ground. It was during this episode that Ramage was wounded.

The fight over Ypres continued for three more years, with more than one and a half million soldiers killed on both sides – equivalent to a third of the Scottish population. But the Germans ultimately failed in their objective and the city became a symbol of Allied tenacity when they eventually broke the deadlock and claimed victory over Germany in 1918.

Inventory: Poisonous chlorine gas. This deadly greenish-yellow gas was first used effectively in war by the Germans at Ypres in April and May 1915. It was either released from a canister to blow on the wind or was launched in a missile. George Ramage was right in the thick of these first attacks.

Protection was primitive. At first, British soldiers used face masks made from flannel cloth soaked in chemicals designed to neutralise the gas. Then came a 'smoke helmet', which covered the whole head. As the war continued, respirators evolved into more effective gas masks similar to those seen during the Second World War.

Fire in the Sea

The enemy was out there, but where?

Sub-Lieutenant Angus Cunninghame-Graham gripped the handles of his periscope and glared at the ocean. The lens was peppered with smoke dust from his own guns and salt-water spray from the enemy missiles which had landed just a few dozen yards away from HMS *Agincourt*'s thinly armoured deck.

Through the muck he scanned the cold, grey sea. He saw dense clouds of mist drifting over thick, foam-flecked waves. Apart from that, nothing.

Then the view cleared a little and there they were – enormous metal monsters, whose fangs and scales were gun barrels and armour plates, squatting in the distance like sinister shadows of the British fleet.

But before the German ships' range could be taken and missiles launched, they disappeared again behind a silvery veil of drizzle.

Cunninghame-Graham cursed under his breath. 'Come on, show yourselves,' he hissed.

BOOM!

A cacophonous explosion shook the *Agincourt* with great violence.

'We've been hit!' shouted one of the men.

Sweat glowed on the faces of the gun-turret crew as they locked their eyes on their commander. Cunninghame-Graham spun his periscope around, seeking signs of damage.

A hundred thoughts swam through his head. Was this it? Was this where his career ended – sunk by a direct hit from a German battleship in the icy North Sea?

Ever since he was twelve years old, when he had started out as a naval cadet, Cunninghame-Graham had looked forward to the chance to do battle. Now his time had come.

For more than eighteen months, almost since the war had begun, he and the rest of *Agincourt*'s crew had been based in the Orkney Islands, off Scotland's north coast. During that time they had prepared meticulously to confront the Imperial High Seas Fleet of Germany's Kaiser Wilhelm II. It had been a long wait, never knowing whether or not their moment would actually arrive.

The *Agincourt* first joined the British Grand Fleet back in late August 1914. When the vessel sailed into the huge sheltered anchorage in the waters of Scapa Flow in Orkney, the place was packed. There were battleships, destroyers, battle cruisers and several other classes of ship – dozens in all.

The ships' vast, silvery-grey hulks were intricately detailed on their upper decks with superstructures, masts, chimneys, rigging, flags, tenders, lifeboats, derricks, platforms, and weaponry – including machine-guns and missile-launching gun turrets.

Lurking below the water lines, out of sight amid forests of

barnacles, were torpedo tubes and huge propellers, the latter powered by immense coal-hungry steam-turbine engines.

The Royal Navy vessels may have been at rest. But not the men who sailed on them. Uniformed figures hurried to and fro under the watching gulls, throwing items overboard or carrying pieces of wooden furniture down the gangways.

Out went tables, chairs, settees and even the portable organs used in the ships' chapels. Anything considered a fire risk in the event of the ship being engaged in battle had to go.

Cunninghame-Graham quietly observed all this activity from the deck of the newly arrived *Agincourt*. He liked the fact that his own captain had refused to take such drastic measures. Throwing furniture and other comforts overboard would only undermine the crew's morale.

At his side was Hoots, his sturdy cairn terrier. The gruff, handsome little dog licked his lips as he watched seabirds landing and taking off from the railings.

Just then, Cunninghame-Graham's attention was caught by activity on his own ship. Further along the deck he could hear pails of water being put down with a clang, followed by sloshing sounds and then scrubbing.

He quietly signalled Hoots to stay put. As he approached the noise, Cunninghame-Graham could see two sailors on their hands and knees with their backs to him, holystoning the decks.

Cunninghame-Graham smiled. This was a job he recalled doing as a naval cadet. Holystoning meant kneeling down and using a small block of rough sandstone to scour the deck's teak wooden planks until they shone a pristine white.

'None of the other ships is doing this, so why are we?' muttered one of the young sailors to the other as he scrubbed away with the salty, wet stone.

'I'll wager none of the other crews get turned out of their hammocks at 5.40 in the morning, either,' grumbled the second lad as he too rubbed and scrubbed with a well-drilled rhythm. 'In that boat next to us they don't wake till 7.15! What a life!'

'Pride of ship is good for morale,' said Cunninghame-Graham.

The two sailors spun around, startled, and instantly stood bolt upright and saluted.

'Aye, aye, sir! Good morning, sir!' they barked in unison.

Cunninghame-Graham, in a swift but relaxed motion, saluted back. 'The captain believes this war's going to be a long one and I think he's right,' he said. 'We'll have to maintain standards if we're going to defeat the Kaiser, will we not?' he added with a smile.

'Aye, aye, sir!'

He instructed them to carry on, then whistled and called, 'Hoots!' Man and dog went below deck to get ready for breakfast.

While the vessel awaited battle orders, all sorts of preparations and methods of killing time were devised. Holystoning was only one of many tasks. The ship was painted and repainted to ward off rot and rust. A pier was built on the barren shoreline of Flotta, a small island inside Scapa Flow off which the *Agincourt* was anchored. And the whole fleet co-operated to build recreational facilities on Flotta, including football pitches and a golf course.

Deck-hockey matches and sailing regattas were held; officers were allowed ashore for shooting and fishing provided they could be back at short notice. Competitions kept everyone on their toes and made sure crews worked together effectively – such as a race to see which crew could be first to deliver a fried egg from their ship to the bridge of the flagship, HMS *Iron Duke*.

Besides fried eggs, food was good and plentiful. One ship was turned into a canteen with a special shop for officers, reminiscent of the exclusive Fortnum & Mason grocery shop in London, where all sorts of luxuries could be bought, from local island lobsters to pâté.

Then there were the serious battle preparations, including target practice. This required the *Agincourt* to weigh anchor and sail into the Pentland Firth, the stormy body of water that lies between Orkney and the Scottish mainland.

Cunninghame-Graham was put in charge of the tugboat that was to be used for gunnery practice.

The *Agincourt's* gunners were supposed to set their aim five degrees off target so that the missiles would land safely astern of the tug. On one occasion, however, a gunner failed to set his aim correctly and his shots began falling dangerously close to the tugboat. Cunninghame-Graham frantically signalled that the firing needed to stop before the tug was hit. Even though the missiles were only practice projectiles, they were filled with almost 400kg of sand and could easily have smashed through the tug's deck.

Three other aspects of naval life in Scapa Flow kept everyone on their toes. One was coaling the ship. Every single officer and seaman, except the captain, took part in this back-breaking task.

Hundreds of bags of coal had to be filled up by hand in the hold of a waiting coal freighter and then hoisted aboard the *Agincourt*. The bags were then emptied down chutes into coal bunkers below deck ready to feed the engine boilers. Sandwiches, lime juice and cocoa kept everyone going until the job was done.

Another challenge was stormy weather. Hurricane-force winds are not unusual in the Northern Isles and the heavy seas often made the *Agincourt's* patrols, when she and other vessels went out into the Atlantic or North Sea in search of any hostile German activity, extremely arduous.

Then there was the fear of being asleep in your hammock or bunk when a German U-boat submarine slipped into Scapa Flow and torpedoed the ship's hull. To ward off such stealth attacks, all entrances to the anchorage had to be kept secure with anti-submarine nets, minefields and patrols.

So there was plenty to keep the crews busy while they waited for their chance to do battle.

Finally, just as hopes were beginning to fade of ever actually facing the enemy, the day came when the entire fleet was ordered to put to sea and sail south-east towards Denmark. Neither Cunninghame-Graham nor the rest of the *Agincourt*'s crew realised it at first, but this was to be more than just another routine patrol.

It was still light at 9pm on Wednesday, 30th May 1916, when the Grand Fleet began steaming out of Scapa Flow. As the last vessels slipped out of the ancient anchorage, the flagship *Iron Duke* took up the rear, lingering as long as possible before breaking telephone contact with the shore in case of new information or a change of orders.

For a short while, wireless radio chatter went to and fro. Messages were sent in cipher – a secret code – and further disguised by a stream of dummy messages. Once the fleet was actually at sea, however, radio silence had to be maintained so as not to give away the ships' positions.

The *Agincourt* was in the 4th Battle Squadron. As she steamed out into the North Sea darkness fell, and Cunninghame-Graham pondered what lay ahead. He also wondered how long it would be before he got soaked to the skin.

Although the *Agincourt* was a state-of-the-art Dreadnought-class battleship and a very steady gun platform, her main deck was extremely difficult to keep watertight in a rolling sea.

As Cunninghame-Graham made his way from below deck towards his battle station for a night watch, his nostrils filled with the stench of stale salt water. All the ventilators had been screwed shut to try to keep as much of the sea out as possible, but this also meant that very little fresh air circulated between decks. He stumbled along in the dark, bending under hammocks with sailors sleeping in them, with an inch or so of seawater sloshing about underfoot.

He arrived wet-footed at his battle station, No. 4 heavy-gun turret. On-duty members of his gun crew saluted and exchanged a few words as they went about their business among the guns and machinery in the turret's cramped compartments.

In the event of battle, everyone had a specialised task to perform. A team of men worked across several decks to bring up the missiles, or shells, from the shell room below.

They also brought up the propellant charges needed to fire the shells from another store down below called the magazine. The shells and the charges were then loaded into the guns.

Meanwhile the sightsetters, directional trainers and gunlayers worked together to lock the guns on target. Everywhere you looked, complex electrical and hydraulic machinery helped make the whole operation run like clockwork.

Cunninghame-Graham felt a certain sense of relief that they were likely to see action very soon. This was what he and the rest of the crew had trained for.

As commander of the turret, he would now spend most of his time here, especially if the *Agincourt* was engaged in battle. He had even had a camp bed rigged up so he could be awoken and ready for action at a moment's notice.

'Look lively, sailor,' he said to one of his foretopmen. The young man had stifled a yawn while looking out of the armoured sighting hood above the guns. 'Don't you know the penalty for falling asleep on submarine watch is to be shot by firing squad!'

'Aye, sir!' came the terror-stricken reply.

'I'm just putting the wind up you,' replied Cunninghame-Graham with a grin. 'You're relieved from watch. Good job. Now go and get some food and rest.'

'Yes, sir!' the young man replied, then, just as he was about to leave, he turned to face his commander. 'Do you think this time will be different, sir?' he asked.

'Do you mean, is this just another false scent, or has the Kaiser's fleet actually been lured out to do battle this time?' replied Cunninghame-Graham.

'Something like that, sir, yes.'

At just twenty-three years old, Cunninghame-Graham knew he lacked the wisdom for an accurate prediction, not having been informed himself yet what was actually going on. The foretopman was not much younger than him, but still he looked up to the officer for some reassurance.

'To tell the truth I have no idea,' Cunninghame-Graham replied. 'But the important thing is to be ready for them, come what may.'

As soon as Cunninghame-Graham had a break, he had an important job to do. He needed to make sure a very special member of the crew was at his battle station, just in case.

'Hoots! Hoo-oots!' Cunninghame-Graham stood at an open hatch, shouting into the half light of the wet breezy deck.

The shaggy little dog was on his sandbox. He looked around with his deep, hazel eyes and barked at his master.

Just then another window hatch opened slightly. 'What the Devil is this racket all about?' came an angry voice from within. 'If I find that blasted dog out there, he's going overboard!'

'Come!' hissed Cunninghame-Graham under his breath, beckoning Hoots with both hands.

Hoots rushed along the deck and into his master's arms.

'We've woken up the Commander again,' whispered Cunninghame-Graham into his old pal's soft, hairy ears as he pulled the hatch shut and clambered down the stairs. 'Let's get out of sight before he catches us.'

Hoots wiggled his black nose and snuffled his agreement.

Down below deck, Cunninghame-Graham gently put Hoots into his 'battle station' – a small compartment where he would be relatively safe.

'So what do you think, Hoots?' whispered Cunninghame-Graham after the dog had settled down to rest on a blanket next to his water bowl. 'Are we going to get a real battle?'

But Hoots was already asleep.

The answer to the question came at 2.30pm the next day. A signal was given from the flagship to raise steam for full speed ahead.

On the bridge of the *Agincourt*, the pilot turned the handle on top of the engine-order telegraph to 'Full Ahead' and a bell rang out from the large clock-shaped device.

This signal from the bridge was electrically relayed down to the engine room, where the order was acknowledged by the handle on their engine-order telegraph being turned to the same position. As teams of muscular sailors in vests shovelled extra coal into the blazing boiler furnaces, the ship surged forward to its maximum speed of 22 knots.

Even though the rest of the crew were cooped up in their individual quarters and could not easily see the bigger picture, they had a good idea what the sudden increase in speed meant.

Half an hour later another signal came from the *Iron Duke*: 'Assume complete readiness for action in every respect!' Orders were then fired off to every part of the *Agincourt* by telephone, telegraph and metal speaking tubes, known as voicepipes.

'*Strike down the hammocks!*' All bedding and other inflammable objects in the cabins and decks were put away as a fire-safety precaution.

'*Rig the hoses!*' This meant hosepipes had to be tied to the decks and turned on so that, in the event of a fire, the water would help douse the flames.

'*Bring up the ammunition!*' Below No 4 turret, and all the others, the shells and propellant charges were removed from the missile stores and magazines, and hoisted up ready for the gunners to use.

At around 3.30pm *Agincourt* intercepted signals that the fleet's battlecruisers, sailing independently of the main fleet, had engaged the enemy.

'This is it,' said Cunninghame-Graham to his turret crew. 'It looks like we're going to get our chance to face the Kaiser's fleet in battle.'

At 4.45pm another signal was communicated around the ship. 'Enemy battle fleet sighted steering north.'

When the gun crew heard this, they all cheered. It was certain now that the Germans had sailed into a fight with the main British fleet – and they were going to get one.

All the gun crews then went for dinner in shifts to make sure every man was well fed and able to concentrate. The crew's canine mascots were also fed and watered. Cunninghame-Graham looked in on Hoots with a piece of fish, which was gratefully devoured. The *Agincourt* and her crew were all set for the fight ahead.

Then, just before 6pm, they closed up to the enemy.

'Action stations!' Every man in the turret's upper and lower decks sprang into position at the sound of this command, poised to load, calibrate and fire the guns.

Cunninghame-Graham put his nose up against his observation periscope at the top of the turret and looked out to starboard. He could see the 5th Battle Squadron, along with the battlecruisers, well engaged in combat – but he could not make out the enemy ships. In the misty weather all he could see was the flashes from their guns and the explosive plumes of spray as their missiles fell around the British ships.

At 6.15pm the remaining British battle squadrons were deployed. The *Agincourt* was ordered, along with all the others, to change course and engage in the fight.

At last the sinister, dark silhouettes of the German High Seas Fleet came into view. The *Agincourt* began preparations to open fire.

A gunnery officer in a lookout post high above No 4 turret spotted one of the enemy ships. He then used a machine called an Evershed to relay the ship's position down to the men in the turret, where the information appeared on a dial.

Cunninghame-Graham and his men checked the position, then rotated the turret so that the gun barrels were pointing in the right direction.

But there was a problem. And it wasn't with the Germans.

Lying between the *Agincourt* and the enemy ship were some British ships of the 1st Cruiser Squadron, apparently intent on glory by taking on the enemy without a thought for the rest of the British fleet. Cunninghame-Graham and his men watched impatiently, trying to work out what was going on.

The funnels and firing guns of the British cruisers were creating so much smoke that it was impossible for the crew of the *Agincourt* to calculate the German ships' range, the distance to target. This information was vital to calculate the tilt of the guns to the correct degree, so that when they were fired the shells would land on the target and not fall either long or short.

As well as being right in the other British ships' line of fire, the 1st Cruiser Squadron's flagship HMS *Defence* almost caused a friendly collision by swinging too close to the battlecruiser HMS *Lion*. At last, the *Defence* and its squadron started sailing out of the way of the British fleet – and straight for the Germans.

'What are they up to, sir?' asked one of Cunninghame-Graham's men, as they watched the scene unfold.

'They're sailing closer to the enemy,' replied Cunninghame-Graham. This was typical of the squadron's wild commander, Admiral Sir Robert Arbuthnot, a thrill-chasing motorcyclist and champion boxer who had a reputation for beating up any members of his crew who disagreed with his orders.

'They're doomed!' cried another man.

He said nothing, but Cunninghame-Graham knew the man was right.

Arbuthnot's mad dash for glory subjected the 1st Cruiser Squadron – whose ships were mostly obsolete and no match for the advanced German battlecruisers and dreadnoughts – to a murderous bombardment.

Cunninghame-Graham and his men watched in horror as missiles rained down on the *Defence*, tearing through her poorly protected decks and striking one of her ammunition magazines, setting off a series of catastrophic explosions. Three of the squadron's four ships – the *Defence*, the *Warrior* and the *Black Prince* – were all sunk, the *Defence* immediately and the others later.

Only the *Duke of Edinburgh* managed to get away. It was later confirmed that around two thousand men, including Arbuthnot himself, drowned in the attack. Many of them were Cunninghame-Graham's friends.

But this wasn't the time to worry about the consequences of Arbuthnot's actions. While the Cruiser Squadron was being blasted out of the way by the Germans, the *Agincourt*'s view became clearer. The enemy was in range and on target. It was 6.24pm.

Switches were pushed, levers were pulled and dials were twisted. Primitive mechanical computers whirred and clunked, and messages were transmitted from station to station. The guns in No 4 turret were sighted and corrected, ranged and trained, until they pinpointed what was reckoned to be the correct spot. Then the final order was given: '*Fire!*'

The order pulsed down electric wires to the Fire Gongs, the two signalling devices next to each gun.

TING! TING! went the metal gongs.

Then a pause.

BOO-BOOM!

There was a bright flash as both 12-inch guns fired. The shells shot into the sky with a monstrous, bone-shaking *ROARRR!* The men knew to leap aside as the huge barrels, each one the length of a Viking galley, recoiled several feet backwards. A sheet of flame momentarily covered the entire length of the *Agincourt* as all fourteen heavy guns fired in unison. The ship shuddered and groaned. Each pair of shells had the combined weight of a motor car, and they raced through the air above the rolling waves at more than twice the speed of sound.

For a few moments Cunninghame-Graham and his men were enveloped in a cloud of smoke that covered their clothes, hair, moustaches and skin in soot. Their ears throbbed.

But there was no time to relax. With metallic clanging, squeaking, scraping and slamming noises, the guns were swiftly reloaded. The deep, thick-toothed cylindrical breeches of the barrels were unlocked and swung open like the doors of bank vaults by men working with slick, well-drilled precision. Cloth bags of cordite – the sweet, nail-varnish-smelling propellant used to fire the missiles – were thrust into the gun chambers, along with two fresh, plump missiles.

TING! TING!

BOO-BOOM! ROARRR!

The turret fired twelve or thirteen salvos like this, with both guns firing each time. Cunninghame-Graham watched through his periscope as the *Agincourt*'s missiles landed around and about what looked like a German Lutzow-class battlecruiser.

The enemy responded in turn. Every now and then Cunninghame-Graham's line of sight was blocked by a sudden wall of seawater and a muffled booming sound as German missiles landed in the waves just short of the *Agincourt*, sending up towering plumes of crystalline froth. If the enemy gunners had calculated the correct range, the *Agincourt* would have been done for.

No 4 turret continued to fire, each barrel now being loosed off one at a time to conserve ammunition. As the fire-control orders came through, Cunninghame-Graham's crew made alterations in the ranging and training of the guns based on their own observations as they hunted for the correct distance that would secure a hit – and hopefully a sinking.

Cunninghame-Graham continued to scan the battlefield, but his view was obscured by smoke and mist. It was impossible to tell whether he and his crew had been successful. Had the enemy battlecruiser been sunk or just disappeared into the gloom, preparing for a new attack?

There was a lull in the fighting. The guns seemed to go quiet, and still Cunninghame-Graham couldn't see much. The periscope lens had become shaded and slimy with smoke dust and spray.

There was some movement, though. He could just make out the grey outlines of the enemy ships emerging from the mist and murk for a few moments, like ghosts, only to vanish again before there was a chance to calculate their position and open fire.

Then came the blast.

BOOM!

It sounded as if the *Agincourt* had been hit. The whole vessel shuddered and shook. There was consternation among the turret crew as Cunninghame-Graham searched with his periscope for signs of damage.

This was the moment he had been dreading, the moment that left him wondering if they were all headed for a watery grave.

'Steady, men,' he said at last, after scouring the length and breadth of the ship. 'We've not been hit. The starboard battery has just opened fire with all ten guns – hence the racket.'

'What's their target, sir?' someone asked.

'Our boys have engaged enemy destroyers closing in to

starboard . . .' He swivelled the periscope round. 'Hang on, we've hit one!'

The men cheered.

'And another!'

But they all knew victory was not yet within their grasp.

The *Agincourt* was soon buffeted again by incoming missiles that mercifully fell either long or short, exploding under the waves and sending thousands of gallons of seawater high into the sky like hellish fountains.

They steamed slowly on past the wreck of HMS *Invincible*, a British battlecruiser that had just been hit. A German missile had slammed into one of the *Invincible*'s gun turrets, piercing its armour and combusting bundles of cordite sticks stored in the turret's magazine.

Like the *Defence* before it, the resulting catastrophic explosion had torn the *Invincible* apart. Its hull was now bottom-up in the icy grey sea. Cunningham-Graham tried not to think about the thousand men drowned or drowning as it sank.

Meanwhile, one of the lookouts at the top of the *Agincourt* spotted something else.

In the gun turret, the telephone rang. 'Torpedo incoming!'

Every man knew what a torpedo strike below the waterline would mean. The gun crew looked at each other, wondering if their luck was about to run out, snared in a deadly trap like a pack of hunted animals. Their cold fear intensified the smell of sweat, seawater, oil and cordite.

Up on the bridge, the captain ordered the *Agincourt* to change course immediately in an attempt to outwit the German attack. Still the underwater menace came at the ship, surging through the waves like a metal sea-monster, leaving a frothy trail behind it.

The *Agincourt* was put under helm, meaning the ship's wheel was spun and locked to make another drastic turn. The vessel tilted sharply. In the cabins and on the mess decks, any crockery or picture frames not lashed down were sent crashing to the floor.

Down in the turret, Cunninghame-Graham and the others held on tight, braced for the impact of the torpedo against the hull.

Then, without any warning, the weapon seemed to run out of power. It surfaced for a moment, then sank without trace.

News of the torpedo's demise rippled across the ship. There were cries of joy and relief. But nerves were soon stretched taut again when a German light cruiser was spotted within range. It had been disabled in an earlier skirmish, yet was still capable of doing the British ships damage.

Cunninghame-Graham's gunners spun back into action and fired off a couple of salvos, then quickly shifted their fire as a much bigger adversary came into view.

All of a sudden the mist had cleared around the vast form of a Kaiser-class battleship – a serious threat, but also a tremendous prize if she could be sunk. Clearly visible at a range of 11,000 yards and closing, she was asking for trouble. No 4 turret gave it to her.

BOO-BOOM!

After a few salvos, Cunninghame-Graham lost the enemy ship for a few moments amid the smoke and spray. He waited until the periscope lens cleared a little and the sea's bulging grey surface came back into view.

Quickly he located the German ship. It was now heading away from them. He peered at his prey, looking for smoke or some other sign of damage. He soon found it.

'I think we hit her,' he said.

'Hurrah!' cheered the gun crew in unison. The exhausted men shook hands, slapped each other on the shoulder and embraced.

Cunninghame-Graham decided to save the celebrations for later. He kept his eyes on the retreating battleship as best he could until, at a range of 14,000 yards, she vanished into the mist.

By now, the periscope lens was almost black.

'I'll take care of it, sir!' said Cunninghame-Graham's range-taker.

He climbed out of the turret and wiped clean the smeared lenses of the periscope and the guns' range-finder, then climbed back inside.

Cunninghame-Graham gave him the thumbs up. He could see more clearly, but there was not a great deal left to see. Night was descending like a shroud.

By 11pm things had quietened down enough for the gun crews to get some relief. Officers and men were sent, two turrets at a time, on a fifteen-minute break to get some food.

Upon their return they witnessed the dying embers of the action. On the *Agincourt*'s starboard quarter, in the distance, the crew could see and hear tell-tale flashes and bursts of heavy firing. But the gaps between the assaults were growing longer.

Cunninghame-Graham could not relax. Instinct told him that day's battle was not yet over, and he was right. There was one last fright. A large ship – the men in the turret couldn't identify it – loomed out of the darkness and passed close by, only to be swallowed up by the night.

Dawn the next morning was calm, bright and misty. Gentle wavelets slapped against the *Agincourt*'s hull as she rocked almost imperceptibly on the light swell. Cunninghame-Graham cast his gaze around the sea to take in the flotsam and jetsam left behind by yesterday's battle.

Floating stark and solid against the two-tone liquid backdrop of ocean and mist were the three other ships in the division – *Marlborough*, *Revenge* and *Hercules*. The rest of the battle squadron – in fact, the rest of the fleet – was nowhere to be seen. The German fleet had vanished too. The remaining four British ships were completely alone.

Cunninghame-Graham had expected to re-engage the enemy at first light and he couldn't help finding the empty sea a sad disappointment.

A torpedo attack had damaged the *Marlborough* and left her unable to sail at speed. So while she limped back to Scotland, the *Agincourt*, *Revenge* and *Hercules* lingered to see if there was any last action to be had.

They didn't have long to wait. Right on cue, a new arrival was sighted. Not on the waves this time, but hanging in the sky above – a Zeppelin airship.

Cunninghame-Graham reacted instantly. Besides being a turret commander he was also the *Agincourt*'s anti-aircraft officer. He quickly manned the ship's only anti-aircraft weapon – a three-inch, twelve-pounder gun, angled high at the sky.

The vast, cigar-shaped German aircraft was still miles away, just a speck in the sky and well out of range. But one lucky strike was all it would take to burst its skin and ignite the hydrogen gas inside, bringing it and its reconnaissance crew crashing down into the ocean in a ball of flame. The temptation was too much.

As Cunninghame-Graham's gun blasted away at the sky, the airship was also spotted by the *Revenge*, which let rip with her own fifteen-inch guns at maximum elevation.

'Nobody's going to hit that Zeppelin at this range, sir!' shouted one of the men.

'No, but we can have some good fun trying!' replied Cunninghame-Graham, to roars of laughter.

Apart from the glimpse of the airship, which got away unharmed, it became obvious that the Germans were now long gone. The High Seas Fleet was on its way back to base in Wilhelmshaven.

The crew of the *Agincourt* felt relief at still being in one piece – the ship had sustained only minor damage – and pride for having acquitted themselves well during the engagement. It was now time to rejoin the Grand Fleet and return to Scapa Flow to prepare to fight another day.

As the *Agincourt* turned to sail home, however, Cunninghame-Graham, like many of the crew members, felt his high spirits evaporate. He looked out on floating patches of oil, ammunition cases, empty lifebelts and other debris which he knew marked the watery graves of thousands of his fellow sailors.

The full extent of the horror was only felt later, back at base in Orkney, where the cold hard facts were revealed. Fourteen ships lost and around six thousand men dead – and that was just on the British side.

In the meantime, there was still an important sailor who needed to be stood down from his battle station and told that the coast was clear.

Cunninghame-Graham went below deck to find Hoots blinking, panting and yapping. The little dog had just survived one of the greatest naval battles of all time, but all that mattered to him was that his master had returned.

WAR REPORT

Personnel: Angus Cunninghame-Graham was born in 1893 and joined the Royal Navy when he was twelve years old. He began his career as a cadet at the junior Royal Naval College on the Isle of Wight, off England's south coast, and was then sent 150 miles west to the senior naval college at Dartmouth, in Devon.

Cunninghame-Graham left college as a midshipman – a junior officer – on board HMS *Vincent*. One of his first jobs was to sit on top of a heavy naval gun and try to make notes about how the gun performed while it went off right underneath him. He did well and was made a sub-lieutenant.

In 1912 Cunninghame-Graham served on HMS *Achilles*, a Warrior-class armoured cruiser. The *Achilles* sailed out into the North Atlantic in April that year – around the same time as the *Titanic* was sunk by an iceberg in the same ocean – and arrived at the archipelago of St Kilda, 110 miles west of the Scottish mainland. The villagers on the islands were starving and Cunninghame-Graham's job was to help deliver supplies of oatmeal, butter, sugar, tea and other humanitarian aid.

When the First World War broke out in 1914, Cunninghame-Graham was posted to HMS *Agincourt* and fought as a gun-turret commander in the Battle of Jutland of 1916. During the war he became very interested in signalling – how ships communicate with each other – and made this his specialism.

During the Second World War he commanded the cruiser HMS *Kent*, escorting Allied convoys in the North Atlantic and Arctic oceans, and protecting them from attack by German U-boat submarines. By the end of the war he was a Rear-Admiral and second-in-command of the British home fleet.

Although Cunninghame-Graham grew up mainly in England, he was a member of a wealthy Scottish landowning family and spent a lot of time in his ancestral homeland. Eventually he inherited the Dunbartonshire estate of his uncle, R. B. Cunninghame-Graham – a famous author, international adventurer and radical Scottish politician.

Angus Cunninghame-Graham's last naval posts were as Admiral Superintendent of the Royal Navy dockyard at Rosyth, in Fife, and as Flag Officer, Scotland – the most senior Royal Navy officer in the country. Thanks to his privileged landowning family background – as well as his own talent, success and loyalty to his Scottish roots – he was made Lord Lieutenant of Dunbartonshire and Keeper of Dumbarton Castle, to which his uniform and wartime medals were donated after he died in 1981.

Event Log: The Battle of Jutland was fought in the North Sea, about 250 miles east of Scotland, on 31 May and 1 June 1916. The battle pitted the British Royal Navy's Grand Fleet against the Imperial German Navy's High Seas Fleet. It was the largest sea battle fought during the First World War, and one of the biggest naval battles in history.

It was also the only time during the war that battleships – the largest and most powerful warships ever built until modern aircraft carriers – were engaged in full-scale combat.

The build-up to the battle began in the summer of 1914, when the war began. The British Grand Fleet was assembled at Scapa Flow in the Orkney Islands. It was positioned there to respond to any attack by the German fleet, which was based at Wilhelmsaven on Germany's North Sea coast.

A thousand years previously the fleets assembled at Scapa Flow were those of the Vikings, Scandinavian raiders from across the North Sea come to conquer northern Scotland in ornate wooden longships propelled by manned oars. Now it was home to ships of such enormous size, technological sophistication and immense firepower as only the Viking gods could have possessed in their time.

After almost two years spent practising, the Grand Fleet's moment finally came. The German fleet, whose masterplan was to seize control of the North Sea, was discovered making an advance out into the North Sea off the coast of Jutland.

The Germans did not intend to face the whole British fleet in battle. They had hoped to lure out the smaller British battle-cruiser squadron, also based in Scotland, from Rosyth naval base on the River Forth and destroy it.

But the Germans' coded communications were broken by the British, who learned about the trap. The entire British Grand Fleet was sent south-east from Scapa Flow in support of the Rosyth battlecruisers, to face the enemy.

The two navies met in a pitched battle, during which 250 combat ships blasted each other for hours with missiles and torpedoes. When the fighting was finally over, the British had lost around 6,000 men and 14 warships – more than double the German losses.

Jutland was seen at first as a German victory, but this view changed over time. The German fleet was forced to return to its base having failed to wrestle control of the North Sea from the British. So the battle was arguably a strategic British victory.

Jutland is a landmass in north-western Europe that reaches out, like a hand, to guard the entrance to the Baltic Sea to the east. Most of Jutland is in Denmark, but its southern section is part of Germany.

The battle was actually fought west of Jutland, in a sector of the North Sea known as 'Fisher'. The area is still mentioned every day on the British maritime weather report, or Shipping Forecast. In recent decades marine archaeologists have discovered the wrecks of ships lost during the Battle of Jutland in an area which is now a protected military grave site.

Inventory: The HMS *Agincourt* was a state-of-the-art Dreadnought-class battleship, built in Newcastle-upon-Tyne and launched in 1913. She was named after the historic battle of Agincourt in which the English defeated the French in 1415.

At over 200 metres long, she weighed more than 30,000 tonnes when fully loaded. She was driven through the water at 22 knots – 25 miles per hour – by four Parsons steam turbines producing around 34,000 horsepower.

The *Agincourt* was defended by fourteen heavy guns mounted in pairs in seven gun turrets. Cunninghame-Graham was commander of No. 4 turret. The barrels of the guns, made by the Elswick Ordnance Company, were each almost 14 metres long and fired explosive missiles weighing almost 400kg each.

The vessel also had six-inch guns – no fewer than 20 – as well as ten three-inch guns. Below the waterline were three 21-inch torpedo tubes, two fore and one aft. In places the ship's armour was up to 12 inches thick, but in other parts of the deck it was only one inch thick, making her vulnerable to a well-placed hit.

Hell's Orchestra

The bombardment had been going on for days. Thousands upon thousands of shells, fired from the barrels of enormous field guns, sailed over the heads of the Scottish soldiers and across the flat French fields.

The shells' explosive impact unleashed hailstorms of earth, rocks and pieces of shrapnel that smashed, tore and burst everything they touched. Bright flashes lit up the sky, followed by tall plumes of grey, brown and blue smoke.

This almighty punishment was being hurled at the Germans by the Allied field guns, preparing the way for the planned ground battle that lay ahead. The aim was to demoralise the enemy, to wreck their trenches, rip open their barbed-wire defences, shatter their guns, flatten their billets and sever their lines of communication. Those soldiers not cut to pieces by shellfire and shrapnel would be left terrified, dazed and confused, their fighting spirit destroyed.

Then, at a time specified by the generals, the guns would cease.

The Allied soldiers would rise up from their trenches, sweep like an avalanche across the German lines and fall on the enemy with bullet, bomb and bayonet.

'May God have mercy on their souls,' said Private William Wilcock under his breath as he crouched waiting for the command. He ran his finger along the blade of his bayonet. It shone dully in the candlelight in spite of the caked-on trench mud. He practised attaching and detaching the bayonet, repeatedly checking that his Lee Enfield rifle and ammunition were in order.

It was Saturday, 25 September 1915 – very early in the morning. Unable to see much in the darkness, Wilcock concentrated on listening. The air was filled with the whoosh and roar of shells flying overhead, and the heavy *CRRRUMP, CRRRUMP* sound of them landing on the German positions. Their trenches lay in front of the French mining town of Loos.

'It sounds like an orchestra,' said Wilcock, turning to a Tommy next to him. He had to raise his voice to be heard above the rumbling din.

'Aye, an orchestra in Hell!' said the other man, curdling a gob of saliva and spitting at the ground.

If Hell is anything like this, thought Wilcock, then it must be a very unpleasant place indeed. He and the rest of his company were huddled on the front line, having spent the previous weeks preparing for the big push while the artillery got on with their work.

With spades, sandbags and spars of wood they had dug and fortified new trenches. These were required to house all the reserves of men who were now swarming towards the front. Everybody knew that numbers were being increased to compensate for the inevitable casualties when the time came for the ground attack.

But for now they had to concentrate on becoming the best soldiers they could possibly be. Through careful training and preparation, each man had learned a specialism that would be vital in making the attack a success.

There were wire-cutters whose role was to snip open the enemy's jagged, tangled defences swiftly and effectively. There were bomb-throwers, or grenadiers, trained to hurl grenades accurately at clusters of enemy soldiers while under fire. The trench-mortar men, operators of small mobile cannons, needed to be swift, precise and cool under pressure. Then there were the Red Cross men, ready to attend to the sick and wounded, and take them to safety.

Wilcock continued checking his equipment. Every so often he lifted his head and ran his eyes up the four-foot-long wooden ladders resting against the wall of the trench. These ladders, which had been knocked into shape in the preceding weeks, then distributed along the trenches, would eventually take him and his comrades over the top.

Wilcock pictured himself clambering up the nearest ladder, over the parapet into No Man's Land and – what then? Would he stride gallantly into the peaceful dim light of early morning or stagger into the murderous glare of enemy artillery? Would he find a lucky opening in the German defences or be caught in a hail of machine-gun fire? Would his advance lead him on to victory or oblivion?

It seemed only a short while since his arrival in France. The people on the streets had shouted '*Vive L'Ecossais!*' – 'Long live the Scots!' – as he and his kilted colleagues marched past. They'd felt, if not quite invincible, then at least confident and optimistic. But now, sitting here in the cold wet trench, he couldn't help wondering exactly how long he had left to live.

He wiped a smear of mud from the face of his watch. It was 4.30am. From what they'd been told, the order would be given to spring into action around 6am. All he could do was wait. He closed his eyes.

'Stand to arms!'

The sudden command roused Wilcock and the rest of the waiting soldiers. His eyes itched with tiredness, but he jumped to his feet, fixing his bayonet onto the end of his rifle in a swift, well-drilled action.

'Prepare to advance!'

Wilcock checked that his tin hat and all the rest of his equipment was in place, and pounced on the trench ladder.

His knees trembled as he climbed the steps. He slithered off the top rung and lay on his belly just beyond the parapet. Like a swarm of ants, dozens more men on either side crawled out too.

This was it.

Wilcock awaited further orders. His packed ammunition pouches bulged uncomfortably against his torso. His heart thumped in his chest. Thick mud oozed against his bare, kilted knees. The whizz, ping, spit and patter of enemy bullets striking hard objects, soft sandbags and damp earth rang in his ears. The enemy wasn't giving up without a fight.

There were screams and whimpers, and bloody gurgling sounds as bullets pierced the flesh and bone of those unlucky enough to be hit before they had a chance to get going. Wilcock kept his head down and prayed he would not be next.

'Company, Advance!'

This was what they'd been trained for. At the command, Wilcock hauled himself up and rushed forward. His senses took in flashing lights, thick clouds of smoke, the *rat-tat-tat-tat* of machine guns, horrifying cries from men struck down and killed or wounded, and barked curses and swearing from those who kept striding forward alongside him.

German shells slammed into the ground all around and the whole battlefield shook. Jagged chunks of shrapnel went whizzing everywhere, but the line of advancing men pushed steadily on, without breaking or buckling.

Suddenly, Wilcock heard a cry. To his left he saw a face contorted in agony. It was a soldier he knew well; a strong man and great fighter who now lay bleeding and shattered in the mud. Wilcock knew the drill. He couldn't pause, couldn't stop, couldn't do anything to help – he could only advance and hope the Red Cross men would help his friend before it was too late.

On went Wilcock through the blinding, deafening maelstrom, amid the swirling smoke. He pushed his way between gaps in the German barbed wire, somehow dodging the relentless enemy fire. He stepped over bodies – some freshly slain; some charred and putrefying after lying in the open for weeks – and splashed round the edges of waterlogged shell craters.

Soon the parapets of the German trenches loomed in front of him. He felt his heart pounding, and he was suddenly giddy with excitement at surviving so far. Roaring like an unstoppable conqueror, he threw himself over a wall of sandbags and into a front-line German trench, finger on his trigger and bayonet at the ready, eyes glaring, looking for someone to kill. Other Tommies poured in alongside him, berserk with war fury.

'Surrender!' yelled Wilcock.

'Give up, Bosche!' barked another Tommy, using a nickname for the Germans.

'*Kapitulieren Sie!*' shouted one of the others, using what little German he knew.

Out of the corner of his eye Wilcock spotted what he assumed was the opening of a large, heavily fortified dugout further along the trench. It probably contained ammunition crates and rations ... but what else? He signalled to his comrades.

One of the Tommies bellowed a warning and threw a grenade inside. In an instant, four Germans leapt out with their hands up. A second or two later the dugout was blown out in a massive explosion that showered everyone with soil, splinters and smoke. The Germans were wide-eyed with terror, their mouths gaping. They surrendered immediately.

Forward went Wilcock and the others – shooting, bayoneting and hurling grenades – until finally they made it safely behind the trenches and ran on into the village of Loos.

The first thing to command Wilcock's attention was the very tall twin-towered steel building which housed the machinery to draw coal up from underground. Next to it was a spoil heap, a gigantic mound of industrial waste created by the coal mine.

Everything else had been smashed to ruins in the shelling. Now, the Tommies had to clear the village of Germans as quickly as they could, take prisoners and try not to harm any surviving local civilians who had not already fled the area.

As Wilcock made his way through the streets, he and a few men from his platoon came upon a house with a badly damaged wall. There was a gash through which they squeezed themselves in order to search the place.

The door to the cellar was locked from the inside, and Wilcock began bashing it with the butt of his rifle. A panel of wood cracked, splintered and then broke apart.

Wilcock squinted through the jagged hole, careful not to make himself a target for anyone with a gun on the other side. But there was only darkness.

Leaning in closer, he took a deep breath of the cellar's damp air and shouted, 'Come out!'

His voice echoed in the gloom. There was no reply.

He looked over his shoulder at his comrades and gestured at the locked bolt on the door. 'There's definitely somebody down there,' he whispered.

They nodded.

He began thinking that a grenade might be necessary, but just then . . .

'*Nous sommes réfugiés!*' A shrill, female voice echoed in the darkness. '*Nous sommes réfugiés!*'

The soldiers exchanged glances. Wilcox recognised the French phrase: 'We are refugees!' They must be locals hiding from the Germans, he thought. He put his head through the opening. 'Okay – come up!' he ordered. He reached his arm through the crack and slid open the bolt to unlock the door.

As he did so, the glow of a lantern appeared in the shadows at the bottom of the stone cellar stairs. Footsteps began shuffling towards them. Wilcock stepped back, the barrel of his Lee Enfield trained on the door. The other men did the same. They couldn't be too careful.

Eventually, the door slowly creaked open. The men found themselves staring into the eyes of a terrified and bewildered-looking elderly woman.

'*Nous sommes réfugiés!*' she repeated quietly and tried to smile, tears streaming down her cheeks. Wilcock gestured for her to move forward and as she shuffled out two other women followed.

'Are you alone?' asked Wilcock.

The ladies looked confused.

He asked again, trying to remember his French lessons. '*C'est tout?* . . . erm, *Vous êtes seuls?*'

'*Ahh, oui – nous sommes seuls!*' the nearest one replied.

One of Wilcock's colleagues looked at him, eyebrow raised. 'What did she . . .?' the soldier began.

'They say they are alone,' Wilcock replied, 'and they're refugees.'

He lowered his firearm and gestured for the others to do the same.

Suddenly the first of the three women rushed at Wilcock and threw her arms around his neck, kissing him on both cheeks and thanking him profusely for not harming them and for driving the Germans out. Wilcock blushed, the other men laughed. They checked out the cellar and the rest of the house just to make sure there were no Germans lurking about.

Unfortunately, there was no time to provide further assistance to the women. The orders were to continue the advance. Wilcock bade them *Adieu* and stepped back outside.

Allied troops were now surging through Loos, waging gun battles on street corners. These usually ended with weary, bloodied and battle-hardened Germans – those who had not fought to the death – being led away as prisoners with their hands on their heads.

Craters pocked the ground where Allied shells had rained down during the previous days. The streets were littered with dead bodies lying in pools of blood and mud.

House after house lay in ruins. Every so often bits of damaged walls would crumble to the ground, sending grey-white clouds whooshing up in ghostly wisps.

Wilcock passed a broken cart lying in a heap, its wheels smashed and axles snapped. It had obviously been laden with the treasured belongings of a local family as they tried to flee from the conflict.

But the attempt had been in vain, and now the contents was strewn about. Wilcock picked his way through furniture, paintings, framed family photographs, clothes, children's toys, broken gramophone records, all sorts of personal items.

The stink was terrible. Bloated bodies of wide-eyed horses and mules lay in heaps, some still tethered to carts and unable to get away fast enough when they bolted in panic. Their limbs were shattered and their bellies burst open. Wilcock tried not to look too closely. Here and there lay other failed means of escape – abandoned bicycles with mangled wheels, broken chains and bent handlebars.

But there was no time to mourn. Wilcock and the rest had to keep going. They marched beyond Loos towards a rise in the ground known as Hill 70, where their objective was to take up a position and dig in.

But the Germans had not given up. As they climbed up the slope, the advancing men came under heavy fire. The shells fell with a scream, a whoosh and a bone-jarring blast. One of them landed right next to Wilcock, the force of the explosion knocking him to the ground. When he picked himself up, he found a lump of hot shrapnel embedded in his rifle.

He didn't have the time to think too hard about it, but his Lee Enfield had probably saved his life. Now it was ruined, the mechanism smashed.

But one of his comrades hadn't been so fortunate. He lay dead, blood pouring from his wounds. The shell had killed him outright, but by a cruel piece of luck his rifle was now Wilcock's for the taking. In seconds the swap was complete.

Exhausted and hungry, the men reached their position and began digging for their lives. The deeper the trench, the safer they were.

But the shells and gunfire kept coming.

A bullet hit Wilcock's spade. Had it struck a few inches further up the shaft it would have taken off his hand.

He looked around, desperate to find something else to help him finish digging the trench. But suddenly his head began pounding in agony. He closed his eyes, wincing at the pain. A few seconds later his stomach was burning.

Unable to control himself, he started vomiting.

'Gas!' somebody shouted. 'Keep your respirators on!'

Retching, Wilcock looked around and saw that the air had turned yellowish-green. Poisonous chlorine. He scrabbled to pull on his primitive cloth gas mask.

He knew he should have been wearing it all along – they had been warned to expect gas attacks – but like many of his comrades, he had found the mask uncomfortable and difficult to breathe through during the advance, and so had taken it off. He regretted that decision now.

As he pulled on the mask, another shell hit the ground nearby and a chunk of flying metal struck him on the shoulder like a hammer. It was a piece of shell casing. Wilcock was very lucky to get away with nothing worse than a nasty, bloody bruise.

As soon as the trench was deep enough, the men stopped digging and hunkered down. This was to be their new front line, well in advance of their old front line back behind Loos. But would they be able to hold it?

'The Huns are coming!' a voice suddenly cried out.

'Stand to arms!' an officer commanded.

Somehow, the Germans had rallied and were now mounting a counter-attack to try to force the Allies to give up the ground they had taken. Fuelled by a burning desire for revenge, they opened fire with sniper rifles, grenade launchers and machine guns. Wilcock and his comrades worked hard to keep them at bay.

Night began to fall and, with it, heavy rain. It grew intensely cold.

Wilcock hugged the top of the trench. With water running off his tin hat, he squinted down the barrel of his replacement rifle, aiming for any Germans he could see through the smoke and rain. Shellfire stung his eardrums, and bullets and shrapnel pitter-pattered all around him, but he was determined not to let his comrades down.

'If we can just hold on until tomorrow,' he told himself as he scanned the murky ridgelines up ahead, 'the reinforcements will get here and we will be able to retire with our heads held high.' After all they had been through, he thought, it would be a dreadful blow if they could not hold their ground for just a few more hours.

Suddenly Wilcock's attention was grabbed by something moving ahead.

'Don't move, Bosche!' he hissed under his breath.

He aimed, squeezed his trigger and the rifle fired, recoiling against his shoulder and spitting out a spent bullet casing with a tiny puff of smoke as he pulled back the loading bolt. Then he thrust the bolt forward again and the spring-loaded magazine pumped another bullet into the chamber, ready to fire.

He loosed off another shot, the ejected bullet casing glancing off his knuckle as he reloaded, and then he fired a few more for good measure. He was as sure as he could be that he had hit a live target, but it was impossible to tell. The air between him and the Germans was a ghoulish, dark broth. You could hardly see a thing.

Somehow Wilcock and his comrades held their position throughout the night. In the morning, just as they had been promised, the reinforcements began arriving.

But it wasn't over yet. A tense day followed as the men waited for the order to vacate the freshly dug front-line trench and hand it over to the incoming troops. Wilcock was beyond tired, his nerves were shattered and his stomach cramped with hunger – they had gone almost two days now without sleep or food.

Eventually Wilcock's platoon was ordered to return to their starting position, leaving others to try to hold the ground that had been gained. They were relieved, but far from safe. Enemy snipers and artillery gunners had no intention of holding their fire so that their exhausted foes could leave unharmed.

Wilcock bent his back and hung his head, trying to make himself less of a target as the bullets whizzed by, and hauled himself out of the trench. His comrades did the same and, one by one, they began streaming back towards Loos.

As they staggered back down the hill under constant enemy fire, several men fell. A soldier near Wilcock was struck by shrapnel and collapsed. He lay prostrate on the muddy ground, unable to move. Wilcock beckoned to another soldier, and together they hauled their wounded comrade to his feet and dragged him to safety – or at least somewhere slightly less hazardous.

Again they passed through the streets of Loos. 'This must be what the streets of Hell look like!' said the wounded man to his saviours, his speech slurred by pain and exhaustion.

Wilcock had to agree. Loos was a scene of carnage, with its twisted ruins and bloody corpses. And yet Wilcock felt a glimmer of hope that if they could just keep gaining ground against the enemy then eventually this terrible war would be won, and villages like Loos would return to peace and normality once more.

At length they returned to where they had come from, mission accomplished. The men of Wilcock's regiment were exhausted. But still they slapped each other on the back, they embraced, they joked and wiped away tears of laughter. They wore their torn and bloodied uniforms and muddy kilts with pride. Everyone knew what they had achieved.

'Let me shake you by the hand,' said a corporal to Wilcock. 'That was bloody well done!'

Even though the big guns still boomed loudly nearby, the men felt comparatively relaxed now and they sat down to eat.

Wilcock dug in to a mess tin filled with meat and potatoes. He felt like a conquering hero returning to a victory feast. He had done his bit to help take a lot of ground from the enemy in the past two days – but his regiment had also paid an extremely high price.

After the meal, Wilcock trooped out of his dugout with the others and they all lined up in the evening light. It was time for the roll call. This was the moment of reckoning, when they found out exactly who had made it and who had not.

There was a pause as the men formed rows. They could all see that their numbers were vastly reduced. Wilcock swallowed hard and braced himself.

A name was called out.

'He's dead, sir!' someone replied, their voice breaking a little.

Another name.

Another trembling response: 'He's dead, sir!'

A third name.

'Missing,' the reply was interrupted by a sob, 'sir!'

And so it went on. Those who had survived unscathed were few and far between. Wilcock grew tearful and saw tears welling in the other soldiers' eyes, too.

The company was inspected by a senior officer. 'Today I want to praise you men for what you have done. You are a credit to the British Empire and to His Majesty the King. And through your gallantry and courage, you have maintained the great name of this fine Scottish regiment.'

A sense of achievement and pride swelled in Wilcock's breast. The officer's words made him feel a little better about the sacrifice of all those who had died. That night, he hunkered down in his dugout and lit a candle. He watched the flame flicker and glow as he reflected on the horror and heroism of war.

WAR REPORT

Personnel: William Raynor Wilcock was a Private in the Gordon Highlanders. During the war he kept a personal memoir in which he charted his experiences, including his arrival in France in the summer of 1915 and his part in the Battle of Loos. He was invalided out of the army in April 1917.

Wilcock came from Leigh, an industrial town in Lancashire, England. It was not unusual for men living outside Scotland to enlist in a Scottish regiment, especially if they had been born in Scotland or had a Scottish parent, or some other connection to the part of Scotland where the regiment traditionally recruited.

Wilcock's Gordon Highlanders were among several Scottish regiments to take part in the Battle of Loos. The others included the Black Watch, the Cameron Highlanders, the Highland Light Infantry, the King's Own Scottish Borderers, the Royal Scots Fusiliers, the Scots Guards, the Seaforth Highlanders, the Scottish Rifles, and the Argyll and Sutherland Highlanders.

Event Log: The Battle of Loos was fought between 25 September and 18 October 1915. The battle was named after a small mining village in the north of France called Loos – pronounced 'Loss'. This battle was the first time the British used poisonous chlorine gas.

Loos is in an area called Artois, about 20 miles south of the French border with Belgium. The battle was part of a bigger plan of attack by the British and French against the Germans. The plan was called 'the Artois offensive'.

At the start of the battle the Germans occupied Loos and the land to the east of it. The British were stationed to the west. So the British objective was to advance east, capture Loos and break through the German lines beyond.

The British had bombarded the Germans with heavy artillery for four days before the actual battle began. Around 250,000 British artillery shells were fired during that time.

Wilcock was part of an advance by Scottish regiments through Loos, which was successfully taken from the Germans, and then on to a bit of higher ground to the east known as Hill 70. The Germans bombarded them while they advanced to Loos and then counter-attacked fiercely when they got to Hill 70. Wilcock's company was eventually relieved by reserves.

The British released 140 tons of gas from canisters on the battlefield. It was supposed to blow towards the Germans but the wind changed strength and direction, and as a result much of it ended up swirling around the British troops. Wilcock was among the many Tommies to be gassed by his own side.

The British were unable to hold the ground gained at Hill 70, so on 28 September they retreated. They tried the attack again in October, but that was unsuccessful too.

In total around 60,000 British soldiers were either killed, wounded or missing as a result of the battle, and a very high proportion of them were Scots. The German losses were far fewer.

Inventory: The Lee Enfield rifle was the British soldier's main weapon during the First World War. It was created in the late nineteenth century by a Scots-Canadian inventor, originally from Hawick in the Scottish Borders, called James Lee.

The Lee Enfield entered service with the British Army in 1895 and was used until 1957. The type used during the First World War was the .303 Short Magazine Lee Enfield, or SMLE, and its nickname was 'the smelly'.

The Lee Enfield was a sturdy and reliable bolt-action rifle. The bolt was a bar with a handle which the gunner slid forward to load the weapon with a bullet and then slid backwards to discharge the spent bullet casing after the gun was fired. The empty bullet casings flew out from the right-hand side of the gun and onto the ground, littering the floors of trenches and dugouts.

In the hands of a skilled infantryman the Lee Enfield could accurately fire up to 15 bullets per minute at a range of up to 600 metres. The rifle had a detachable bayonet, or short sword, for attacking the enemy in hand-to-hand combat.

More than 15 million Lee Enfields are thought to have been manufactured. The gun is still used by some armies and sports shooters today.

A Hasty Retreat

A red glow on the skyline confirmed that the enemy would soon be upon them. Villages just a few miles away were on fire. Every now and then there was a flash, each one seeming closer than the last, followed by louder and louder booms as the big German field guns launched their missiles before being hauled ever nearer.

'Attention please! The order has been given to retreat! The tents and equipment must be packed away immediately!'

The announcement startled Mary Milne, whose mind had been full of meat and vegetables. As the field hospital's cook, she was contemplating the next day's menu for the hard-working and hungry staff. She had become quite used to the distant noise of battle.

'Everybody must be ready to leave in the morning!' There was no mistaking the commanding tone of Dr Inglis. She was the founder of the Scottish Women's Hospitals and leader of this particular mobile unit treating wounded soldiers in Romania, on the war's eastern front.

For the past few weeks the hospital unit had been camped on a relatively tranquil hillside overlooking the pretty medieval town of Medgidia. Now that tranquillity was shattered.

Milne was soon working feverishly with the other women, helping to pack up the whole camp so that it could be transported to a safer place further north.

Very soon there would be no Allied soldiers left to treat here anyway. The combined army of Russian, Romanian and Serbian troops was retreating. They were being pushed back by an enemy force of Bulgarians and Germans.

Even the weather had turned nasty. Lightning flashed and thunder rumbled around the hills. As Milne and the others worked in the dark to uproot tent pegs, crate up medicines and surgical instruments, and fold away stretchers and bedding, they were drenched by lashing rain. Women scurried to and fro, splashing through muddy puddles, working in the glow of hurricane lanterns.

'You'd think we weren't welcome here any more,' said a medical assistant with a grim smile as Milne helped her take down a tent, rainwater running into their sleeves and along their shivering arms.

'Yes, it's become rather a weird scene,' replied Milne. She pushed her soaking hair out of her face as another flash from the heavens bathed the emptying campsite in electric-blue light while thunder and cannons boomed. On she worked, through the night.

In the morning, the sun rose from the Black Sea to the east. The storm had passed and the day dawned clear and bright, but still the guns boomed louder.

While the women waited to leave, they sat or lay on the stone steps of the old Romanian military barracks next to which their tents had been pitched, looking out on the remains of their camp. Some were reading scraps of newspaper, others flicked through photographs of friends and family.

Some wrote entries in their diaries: 'Sunday, 22 October 1916 – time to leave our beautiful camp on the hillside . . .'

'The enemy must be in the garden by now,' said Milne, only half joking, to a nurse who was standing next to her looking through a pair of binoculars.

'Yes, someone ought to go over there and tell them to kindly be quiet since Dr Inglis is sleeping,' came the reply.

Suddenly an aeroplane appeared in the sky, followed by two more. 'They're not friendly,' said the nurse with the binoculars. 'Quick, everyone inside!'

They took shelter just as the enemy aircrews began dropping their bombs. The missiles came whistling down and exploded, embedding chunks of shrapnel in walls and trees.

The building rumbled and shook, glass windows shattered. For about ten minutes – it seemed like ten hours – all Milne and the others could do was to pray they would survive the attack. They cheered when Russian and Romanian planes appeared in the sky and chased the marauders away.

At last the evacuation began. At 11.30am a large group of staff, including several sick or injured nurses and assistants, was taken away on a hospital train, which had already been loaded with baggage and equipment.

The ultimate destination for the whole unit was a city called Galati, 120 miles north at the delta of the River Danube. To get there, it was decided that they would have to make the journey in stages, travelling independently in groups.

While several groups made an early departure, Milne and some others waited behind with Dr Inglis. They would travel to Galati via places where they could provide some help for wounded soldiers. Dr Inglis had decided that their first stop would be Karamurat, to the north-east of Medgidia. She expected that retreating Allied soldiers there would be in need of medical attention.

While they waited for their transport, Milne prepared a meal for her colleagues consisting of black bread and cold meat, with tea made on a Tommy Cooker – a portable stove.

Finally, a lorry arrived to take the remaining crates of equipment. This meant the last few staff could get going too, before the place was overrun by enemy troops.

The lorry, driven by a local guide, was loaded up with the medical equipment plus seven hospital staff and then set off. Behind it drove a Scottish Women's Hospitals staff car containing Milne, Dr Inglis and a couple of others. Taking up the rear was a hospital ambulance containing the last few staff and what little food they had left.

Just as they were leaving the deserted streets of Medgidia, the lorry tore around a sharp corner and a stretcher fell off. Milne's car stopped to pick it up and the ambulance halted too.

'Oh, blast it!' exclaimed Dr Inglis, as the lorry disappeared in a cloud of dust, unaware that it had shed some of its precious load. 'We've lost sight of our guide.'

It was impossible to tell which turning the lorry had taken so they stopped to ask directions to Karamurat from some retreating Allied soldiers. Some of them spoke English, but with others it was better to try German – even though that was the language of the enemy. It soon became clear that they were heading in the wrong direction.

Just as they were setting off again, a boy hopped aboard the footplate of the car. He gestured that he would show the way.

'Karamurat!' he shouted, tapping his chest then pointing at the road ahead.

The women gratefully accepted his offer. With the boy hanging onto the side of the car and pointing the driver this way and that, along shortcuts that took them through gorgeous scenery bathed in a red and gold sunset, they made their way slowly towards their destination.

Just before they turned on to the mountain road that would take them into Karamurat, the boy hopped off the footplate with a wave. Milne watched him disappear in a cloud of dust. They drove on as night fell and the rain began, but the road was good.

After a while their headlights revealed groups of people and what looked like vehicles coming towards them. There was a steady stream at first, but soon the numbers increased until the anxious travellers clogged up the road.

The hospital car and ambulance squeezed past enormous horse-drawn carts and caravans. They looked like small mobile houses, piled high with people, their possessions and their caged farm animals – including pigs, sheep and hens. Most of the carts were pulled by cream-coloured oxen.

'These poor people look thoroughly miserable,' said Milne as she looked out into the wet night.

Peering back at her from where they lay on mattresses in the carts were elderly people too sick or frail to walk. Huddled next to them were terrified-looking children.

Men accompanied their families on foot. They shouted, pushed and shoved at each other as they jostled to make way for the motor vehicles.

On the heels of the civilians came waves of Romanian soldiers. Some were marching, many were walking wounded, and a number were on horseback. Some horses towed cannons or military wagons, others pulled Red Cross carts containing the more severely wounded soldiers.

Eventually the car and ambulance were forced to halt, and Milne and the others took the opportunity to get out and ask directions.

'How far to Karamurat?' Milne asked one of the passing Romanian officers.

He looked her up and down, baffled by her uniform and tartan tie. But he was in a hurry, so he simply pointed over his shoulder. Behind him in the distance Milne could see the glow of a burning village.

'You see that?' he said grimly. 'That is what awaits you if you do not turn back.'

He was about to leave when Milne caught his arm and explained that they were nurses, and that there might be wounded soldiers at Karamurat in need of treatment.

The officer shook his head sadly. 'Karamurat is over there,' he said, pointing now in a slightly different direction at some twinkling lights in the distance. 'Follow the road and it will take you. But just look around,' he added, opening his arms wide. 'Everyone is fleeing from the Germans and the Bulgars, even the soldiers. Turn back while you still can.' And with that, he left.

When Milne went to pass the information on to Dr Inglis she could tell from her boss's expression that turning back was not an option. 'We need to set up a dressing station for wounded soldiers,' said the doctor firmly, 'and we can't just abandon the girls in the lorry. They've probably already reached Karamurat.'

Milne climbed back into the car, and the two vehicles continued, edging their way through the oncoming refugees.

The town of Karamurat was dark and appeared almost empty when they arrived. The only signs of life were soldiers sitting miserably in groups trying to keep warm around campfires. There was no sign of the lorry or the other hospital staff anywhere. They drove around for a while before they noticed a faint light coming from one of the houses.

'Mary, you are our good German speaker,' said Dr Inglis, turning to Milne. 'I need you to start knocking on doors to find out what has happened to our missing girls.'

'Yes, Dr Inglis,' replied Milne, and she hurriedly pushed open the car door. She was the youngest member of the group and glad of an opportunity to impress Dr Inglis.

But the first thing Milne did was slip in the mud and fall on her face. Her limbs were so cold and stiff after hours of bone-shaking driving in the car's wet and windy cabin that she was barely able to stand. Slowly she got to her knees and then her feet, shaking and rubbing herself vigorously to loosen the mud and warm her muscles. She glanced back at the car.

Dr Inglis made a shooing motion with her hand. 'Go on, girl, go on,' she said.

Milne walked slowly up to the house until she stood in front of the door. Nervously, she raised her hand and was just about to knock when the door opened.

A few minutes later she was back at the car window.

'Look who I've found,' she said, smiling brightly in the darkness. 'His name is Viktor.'

Viktor was a Serbian soldier. He spoke German and had agreed to try to help find the missing girls.

'He says he can take us to the Red Cross Station, which is quite near,' said Milne. 'They'll know where our nurses are.'

'Good girl,' said Dr Inglis. 'We will wait for you here.'

When Milne and Viktor arrived at the Red Cross Station, they were met by a very unfriendly matron who gruffly told them she knew nothing. 'You should try looking for your friends at the Serbian headquarters,' she told them, as she showed them out.

'I know a shortcut,' said Viktor. 'It's not far.'

Soon the two of them were sneaking through gardens full of sleeping soldiers, sprinting across courtyards full of horses, and crawling through fences in which they had to tear holes to get to the other side.

'This is some shortcut,' muttered Milne, as she tried to keep up with Viktor.

Eventually they came to a sheer wall. Milne glared at Viktor, who admitted he must have taken a wrong turn somewhere. The only way to get back on track was to climb the wall, he assured her. Grunting with exertion, Viktor lifted Milne as high as he could and finally she managed to hook her fingers over the top of the wall and pull herself up.

When the pair were both perched atop the wall, the young soldier jumped into the darkness on the other side and landed with a splash.

Bracing herself, Milne lowered herself as far as she could and then let go. She too landed with a splash. But it was the smell that appalled her. 'It must be an open sewer,' she thought to herself, wondering what she must look and smell like now.

But Viktor was undaunted. 'Come on!' He grabbed her by the arm and they set off once more.

Eventually they reached a dark courtyard with a door. Viktor slipped inside and disappeared. Milne stood alone, waiting for his return. She was intensely hungry, cold and miserable. Her body stank. She wanted to run away, but where could she go? She had no idea how to get back to the car. If Viktor didn't come back, she had no idea what she would do.

Finally he reappeared. 'This way!' He beckoned her inside.

Milne was taken swiftly down a passageway and pushed through a doorway into a dimly lit room. The door closed behind her. In front of her were three older men, one half dressed and the other two lying in bed. A feeling of dread tugged at her stomach. Was this a trap?

The half-dressed man spoke to her in German. 'Please excuse us,' he said. Something about his tone of voice reassured Milne. He smiled wearily. 'We weren't expecting a visitor and had already retired for the night. We are all leaving Karamurat at four in the morning.'

He explained that they were Serbian officers and that they knew nothing of the whereabouts of the seven Scottish women. 'Perhaps you should try the Russian headquarters.'

Milne thanked the men and wished them well. She and Viktor set off for the Russian HQ. But nobody there had any news of the missing girls.

'We are leaving here – and so should you,' said a tired-looking General. He was surrounded by men bent over desks, writing reports, tracing troop movements on maps and answering telephones that rang constantly. 'The enemy will be here in the morning and this is no place for women,' he continued. 'But go to the Romanian headquarters if you have not been there already. They might know something about your friends.'

There was no luck at the Romanian HQ. No courtesy either. Well-dressed young officers mocked the bedraggled and strange-smelling foreign woman in their midst, with her crumpled tartan tie and grey shirt, muddy waterproof coat and boots, her tangled wet hair plastered to her scalp.

Milne fumed but tried to hide her anger. Eventually, an older officer who had been studying a map on a wall pushed Milne's tormentors away and repeated what the Russian General had told her. 'We are leaving and so should you. This is no place for a woman!'

Exhausted and demoralised, Milne asked Viktor to lead her back to the car. This time he took no wrong turns.

'My dear girl, we thought we had lost you too,' cried Dr Inglis, when they returned. 'Where have you been?'

Milne explained what had happened. 'Nobody has seen anything. I don't think the lorry can ever have arrived in Karamurat,' she said. 'I'm sorry, Dr Inglis.'

'Nonsense,' said Dr Inglis. 'You have done well. We now know for certain they are not here yet, so we shall just have to wait for them to arrive. We need a roof over our heads.'

Viktor led them all to the Serbian HQ, where he arranged accommodation for them while they waited for their missing companions. Milne thanked him for his help and off he went into the night. Meanwhile, they were told to wait while an officer arranged a room for them to sleep in overnight, but he insisted that there was no food available.

'Officer, we have eaten nothing since this morning and it is now near midnight,' said Dr Inglis in her commanding Edinburgh accent. She glared at the man. 'There *must* be some food here.'

The officer shook his head and went away grumbling.

Finally, the women were led along corridors lined with sleeping soldiers to a room with straw bedding and green blankets. Basins of water, towels and soap were brought in. Milne washed, relieved to get rid of the stench from the sewer, then lay down in the straw and slept.

After an hour they were woken by a knock at the door. In came soldiers carrying plates of food – Russian soup, roast turkey, bread and tea.

Astonished, the women sat up and tucked into their feast while a satisfied Dr Inglis announced, 'There, isn't this much better?' Milne smiled to herself as she chewed. If Dr Inglis wanted something for her people, she got it.

At dawn, the Serbian officer who had provided the meal came to say farewell. 'We have to go, I'm afraid,' he said. 'If the enemy catches us, we won't be taken prisoner, we'll be shot. They are very near. You too should . . .'

'Yes, yes, officer – we shall be going as soon as possible,' interrupted Dr Inglis. 'This is no place for a woman, and so on.' She winked at Milne. 'We thank you for your help, and rest assured,' Dr Inglis continued, 'since there is no work for us to do here we will not be delayed for a second longer than is necessary. I wish you and your men good luck.'

With that, the officer left. Dr Inglis then turned to the others and said, 'As soon as our missing girls turn up, we'll get out of here. I cannot consider leaving without them.'

Soon afterwards, at around 6am, a courier on a motorcycle arrived bearing good news. The seven missing staff were safe and well, but had been delayed. They were awaiting new orders from Dr Inglis.

The news cheered and relieved them all, and Dr Inglis

immediately reorganised the group for the onward journey. They had to act quickly. The guns of the enemy were booming louder.

Luckily, the Serbian army had not yet completed their withdrawal so a lift on some horse-drawn army carts was arranged for Milne and a few others. They were instructed to make their way to a place called Gradina. Meanwhile Dr Inglis and the rest of the group would take the motor vehicles and drive along a different road in order to link up with the seven missing girls, and then rejoin Milne and the others as soon as possible.

Milne squeezed herself and her haversack of belongings in among the straw on the back of one of the carts. She waved goodbye to Dr Inglis and the others as the grey cart-horse clip-clopped down the street.

Craning her neck as she tried to get comfortable, Milne saw they were approaching a building that towered over the others. On its flat roof was a lot of activity. A huge group of soldiers were looking intently into the distance, pointing and arguing.

Suddenly there was panic. A roar went up as the soldiers ran off the roof and down the stone steps that clung to the outside wall of the building. Onto the street they fled, past the carts carrying Milne and her companions. Though it wasn't a language she knew, it was not hard to get the jist of their cries.

'The Bulgars! The Bulgars!' screamed a wild-eyed young soldier as he pelted down the road, clutching his rifle. He was just one of scores of men shouting.

All of a sudden there was a huge explosion. An enemy shell landed nearby and set a building on fire. Then another shell struck, followed by another. Soon the whole place was under heavy bombardment and house after house caught fire, creating a raging inferno.

Children and their parents streamed out of doorways and alleys where they had been hiding and ran down the middle of the street. The retreating soldiers charged ruthlessly among them, knocking down youngsters and the elderly in their eagerness to escape.

Milne watched in horror as a cavalryman on a charging horse got tangled up in a dangling telegraph wire. The wire pulled tightly against his torso and he was flung to the ground with an agonised scream.

Other terror-stricken soldiers, desperate to avoid being trapped in the town, clawed at the sides of Milne's cart. One of them tried to haul himself aboard, but she tore at his fingers and beat him off. The horses simply could not carry any greater burden with such a long and uncertain road ahead.

Another shell landed with a whoosh and a *BLAAAST!* sending debris flying. A new fire began raging.

'Get us out of here, for God's sake!' shouted one of the nurses.

The lead driver cracked his whip and snarled at the horses, who began galloping through the crowd. With a teeth-chattering shake and rattle they flew down the road.

CRASH! A wheel hit a pothole. *THUNK!* Another slammed into a rock, bouncing the cart high and almost rolling it over. The women clung onto each other and prayed.

Out beyond the boundary of the town they charged, alongside the fleeing mass of people. They crossed railway bridges and rivers, galloped over moors and fields, climbed steep hills and passed through clusters of houses where the only living souls were stray dogs and abandoned farmyard animals.

Some of the sights Milne saw horrified her – yet she couldn't help but look. An ox, too weak to drag a cart out of a muddy field, was being whipped relentlessly while the owner's wife and children huddled, crying in the back. Eventually the crazed man grabbed a sword from a passing soldier and slashed his poor beast with the blade.

Elsewhere an officer threw a woman and child off the back of their cart so he could have it for himself. Milne was relieved to hear later that the pair had been picked up by others and carried to safety.

The stream of refugees thinned as the women's carts got ahead of the crowds. Eventually they made their way through a narrow pass and down into the valley beyond. There lay their destination – the village of Gradina.

The women were invited to camp with a Serbian military medical unit that had left Karamurat earlier. The exhausted horses were unharnessed, fed and watered. The women washed as best they could. They were offered a meal by some Serbian army officers. Milne wolfed down the tasty hot soup, roast lamb and cabbage.

They had only a brief rest before a motorcyclist arrived with a stark message from Dr Inglis. They were to leave Gradina at once and should prepare to travel all night. By now the weather had closed in, and they set off into the cold and dark. Milne cursed her rain-soaked coat.

After making a number of wrong turns they found themselves travelling alongside the Serbian medical unit, which had also retreated from Gradina. The booming guns of the enemy – still advancing – made it easy to see why.

Exhausted, but unable to sleep, Milne was sitting hugging her freezing knees when she heard a shout coming along the line of a hundred or so carts.

'Halt! Motor cars behind us!'

Milne turned and peered into the darkness. It was the car and ambulance carrying Dr Inglis and her group. Soon the grunting vehicles with their glowing headlamps came alongside, and the cart-travelling nurses were reacquainted with the more modern form of transport. As Milne gratefully took a slug of brandy from the ambulance driver she was relieved to be told that the seven staff in the lorry had been met and sent on to safety further north.

Eventually they came to a river where the bridge was in a very poor state. Pedestrians and horses could only just pass over the rickety structure. The exhausted drivers of Dr Inglis's convoy were adamant that it was not safe to try to cross it with the car and ambulance in the dark.

Dr Inglis assessed the situation for a moment, then nodded. 'We shall camp here by the roadside until morning.'

The Serbs who were retreating alongside them thought that camping by the river in the open, in late October, with the enemy advancing, was madness. They begged Dr Inglis to reconsider, but her mind was made up. One of them offered to stay, but the rest of the Serbians reluctantly continued across the bridge and left the Scottish women to it.

Milne set to work, prepared a fire and then cooked a meal for them all. After they had eaten they lay down, wrapped in their blankets, and chatted.

They were interrupted now and then by passing groups of soldiers and refugees, who would simply stand and stare, then wander off. At one point, some women came and asked for food, and the nurses gave them what leftovers they had.

Although it was good to be together again, there was no

possibility of relaxing completely. They were all too aware that the enemy was hard at work some miles distant, fringing the skyline with fire and filling the night air with the faint *CRUMP! CRUMP!* noise of their guns. But they ignored it as best they could. The heat of the crackling campfire soon made them drowsy and eventually their chattering voices fell silent and they slept.

When Milne opened her eyes, she checked her watch in the early morning light. It was five o'clock. 'Time to find breakfast!' she announced to her yawning colleagues. She tossed a fresh branch on the smouldering fire and hung up a pitcher of water to boil. Then off she went, wondering what she might find.

Passing through a beautiful forest of ferns and yellowing trees, she came upon a thatch-roofed village. The broad road had houses on either side, but the whole place seemed absolutely deserted. She entered the first farmyard she came to.

A large, muscular black dog with a white chest darted towards her, snarling. It was flanked by two more, growling and howling. The dogs barked at the tops of their lungs, two circling her, one springing up and down, all with saliva dripping off their bared teeth. Milne stood there unable to move.

Just then a door opened at the far side of the courtyard. A woman's face slowly peered round it. The dogs' aggression lessened slightly. Milne took a deep breath and marched straight up to the door.

The woman retreated but did not quite shut the door. Milne could not speak Romanian, so she tried a bit of French. There was no response, so instead she tried German.

'Are you a German?' came the reply from behind the door. The dogs continued crowding Milne's heels.

'No,' Milne replied. 'We are fleeing from the Germans and the Bulgarians. We are the Scottish Women's Hospital from Great Britain. I just want to buy some eggs, if you have any.'

There was whispering behind the door and then slowly it was opened. A large group of women streamed out into the courtyard. The dogs melted away. One of the women explained that they were in hiding because some 'friendly' retreating soldiers had raided the village.

'There is not a man left in the village apart from three very old ones,' she said.

'The soldiers came and looted everything in sight,' said another. 'Our horses, oxen and cows.'

'One of them came to me and stuck his bayonet in my ribs, demanding bread,' said a third woman.

In the distance they could hear the boom of the guns. 'The enemy is coming,' said the first woman, pointing. 'We cannot get away. Without horses and carts we could walk, but our children can't.'

Milne felt utterly dejected. She had arrived in the village with a spring in her step, but now she was crushed, knowing there was nothing she could do for these poor women.

'Please, Miss, do you have a charm for my child?' A young woman cradling a baby at her breast looked at Milne with a mixture of fear and hope.

Milne took out a threepenny piece which she had carried with her ever since she was a little girl. 'Here, take this,' she said to the young mother. 'Do you see the head of Queen Victoria on one side? That side must be worn facing outwards.'

The young mother turned the coin over and over in her hand, her eyes filling with tears.

'Good luck,' said Milne.

The women quickly gathered food for her. Clutching jugs of milk, a big bag of eggs and a loaf of bread, Milne returned to the camp.

After breakfast, they convoy got going. The drivers gingerly nursed their vehicles over the ramshackle bridge, then attempted an ascent on the steep hill at the other side. They had to go at it with all the power and momentum they could muster, as the slope was caked in mud. Finally they made it to the top.

During the journey that followed, Dr Inglis decided the group would make for a town called Harsova on the bank of the River Danube. From there, they would sail by barge to the safety of Galati.

Harsova was a beautiful, ancient harbour town with a castle built during the Roman Empire and many other fine buildings. But it had been heavily bombed and virtually every structure was damaged in some way.

'All of the windows are shattered,' observed one of the women as they drove through the streets towards the port. The vehicles' chuntering petrol engines echoed against bomb-blasted walls. Finally the road opened out onto the quayside.

Some other members of the unit who had made their own way there from Medgidia were waiting by the water's edge to make the final leg of the journey. The lorry and its seven passengers had already left on a barge that morning and was now on its way to the safety of Galati.

Milne couldn't wait to join them. It had been a long and exhausting few days. The General in charge of loading the barges explained that the town was being completely evacuated, so if they wanted a safe passage they had better leave that night.

But Dr Inglis had other ideas. Instead of sailing to Galati right now, she told the General that she had decided to take a few staff with her in the hope of linking up again with the Serbian medical unit. 'They will be in need of our help,' she briskly told the exasperated General, refusing to heed his instructions for her to join the evacuation.

Eventually he gave up. 'Fine!' he said angrily, throwing his hands in the air, and turned to an officer, ordering, 'Fill the next barge with soldiers only!'

Milne watched, dismayed, as Dr Inglis tried to make the necessary arrangements. It became clear there was no petrol to refuel the vehicles, nor any horses, and she was forced to abandon her plan. Dr Inglis was not used to being thwarted, but she cheered up when a Romanian doctor assured her that a dressing station was urgently required where they stood, on the quayside in Harsova. Wounded soldiers from the nearby battlefront would soon be pouring in, he said, and would need treatment for their injuries before being evacuated along the river.

'We can't all stay,' Dr Inglis told her staff. 'They can only accommodate two doctors and two nurses in case they need to get us to safety quickly.'

'The rest of you must leave tonight by . . .' She frowned at the barge as it was being loaded and paused, perhaps wishing she hadn't rubbed the General up the wrong way. 'By any means available,' she finished.

Milne was relieved that she hadn't been chosen to be part of Dr Inglis's small team. She could finally head for Galati and safety. But there was still a major – and bad-tempered – obstacle. Would the General allow them to travel on the next barge?

They decided to send two of the prettiest girls in the group to try to charm him. The girls returned with news that he would do what he could. They had no choice but to wait patiently.

Milne cursed the cold and hunger as she wandered up and down the quayside watching barges being loaded with equipment, vehicles, horses and soldiers. If only Dr Inglis wasn't always so determined! The noise of cranes winching, heavy weights banging and thudding, and men shouting filled the air. Eventually the order came. The Scottish women would be permitted to board the next barge.

But at the last minute there was yet another problem. There was not enough space on the barge for two of the hospital vehicles and the drivers refused to leave without them. Milne and the others didn't want to leave their two friends behind. They had been through so much together.

'Look,' said an officer, 'the rest of you had better go now while you have the chance. It will be much easier to get the two stragglers away later. If you insist on staying, there is a great risk we won't have space left for any of you.'

Milne reluctantly agreed and took charge of the main group as they boarded the barge. They stood on the deck and looked on as their two friends paced up and down in front of their cars on the quayside.

Finally, at around two o'clock in the morning a new order was issued. The drivers and their vehicles were loaded after all.

Although relieved, Milne could not yet relax. It would be a couple of days before they reached Galati and the dark, cramped barge contained new dangers. Some of the soldiers on board were behaving like a pack of animals, swarming around the car and constantly trying to get in. Terrified at what the soldiers might do to them, Milne and the others spent the night batting them away. But rowdy soldiers weren't the only problem. Occasionally one of the horses, nervous and stressed, got loose and caused mayhem.

Sleep was impossible. That night the barge hardly moved except to make way for other vessels to access the quayside. It was not until daybreak that they finally got going.

The morning was bright and sunny as the women looked out from the deck. The 'beautiful blue Danube', as it was known from the famous waltz, was exactly that. The barge sailed past pretty thatched villages with white stone churches. Orchards and grassy slopes stretched away into the distance, grazed by hundreds of horses. The war seemed miles away.

The soldiers calmed down a little. In the clear light of day the men seemed to accept that the medicine women in their midst had been through the wars too. They were just as shattered with nervous and physical exhaustion as the men, and deserving of some respect.

A Russian driver brought Milne and the others some vodka. Later, while they put in to a harbour where the barge was unloaded and reloaded, the captain brought them some bread, sugar and boiling water to which they added some cocoa that miraculously they still had with them. Gradually the women were able to relax.

The good weather didn't last long. It started to rain and the docks stank. During the night, off went much of the cargo and the horde of soldiers. In the morning, on came a host of sick and wounded. The women got to work as best they could.

'Mary, can you finish dressing this man's wound for me?' said one of the nurses, handing Milne the end of a bandage.

The soldier was sitting on the deck, bloody and battered,

propped up against a pile of equipment and the backs of the other wounded men next to him. He seemed amused at Milne's dishevelled uniform as she nursed him. When she was finished, he grunted his thanks.

At last, on 26 October, they arrived in the safe haven of Galati, where they were welcomed by the British Red Cross and re-united with their colleagues. Eventually Dr Inglis too reached Galati and – with characteristic determination – immediately began to set up a Scottish Women's Hospital Unit there.

Sitting at the edge of the beautiful blue Danube and reflecting on their adventure, Milne wrote in her diary: 'We have only been in Romania for a short while, but between 22 and 26 October 1916 we seem to have lived a lifetime.'

WAR REPORT

Personnel: Mary Lee Milne played an active and varied part in the First World War. She worked as a cook, translator, messenger and junior group leader with the Scottish Women's Hospitals for Foreign Service, an organisation founded by Dr Elsie Inglis. She was highly regarded by Dr Inglis, who raised her to the rank of officer, and she recorded her experiences of working for Dr Inglis in her journal.

Dr Inglis, who lived most of her life in Edinburgh, was one of the first generation of female doctors in Britain. She was also a campaigner for women to have the same rights as men by voting in elections and having a career.

The First World War gave Dr Inglis the chance to combine her medical and political passions. She persuaded the Scottish

Women's Suffrage Society to support the creation of a new organisation – a group of medical units to treat soldiers on the war's front lines, staffed and run entirely by women.

The government's War Office, which was run by men, rejected the idea. But through private donations and fundraising, Inglis's plan came to fruition – and the result was the Scottish Women's Hospitals.

The organisation's headquarters was in Edinburgh, with branches in Glasgow and London. Units were sent out to locations on the western and eastern fronts of the war – such as France, Serbia and Russia. The Scottish staff was joined by women from many countries, England in particular.

Dr Inglis led her organisation from the front, which is why she was running the unit in Romania in which Milne served. Dr Inglis died of cancer in 1917 at the age of just 53 and was buried in Edinburgh, but the work of the hospitals she created continued until the end of the war.

Event Log: The events in this story take place in 1916 in Romania, a country in Eastern Europe next to the Black Sea. This area formed part of the Eastern Front of the First World War.

In August that year, Romania entered the war on the side of Russia and the Allies. As a result Romania was attacked by the enemy side, known as the Central Powers, which included armies from Germany and Bulgaria – Romania's southern next-door neighbour.

The Scottish Women's Hospitals unit went to Romania to help the Allies. Specifically, they went to give medical assistance to a division of volunteer soldiers from Serbia who were fighting alongside the Russians and Romanians against the Germans and Bulgarians in Romania's south-eastern corner.

In late October 1916, the German and Bulgarian armies advanced from the south and forced the Allies north to the delta of the River Danube. The Scottish Women's Hospitals unit was compelled to join the chaotic Allied retreat alongside hundreds of thousands of refugees.

During the year that followed, Russia pulled out of the war and Romania was surrounded and crushed for a time by the Central Powers. However, in 1918 the Central Powers were defeated by the Allies and Romania finally emerged victorious.

Inventory: Before the First World War, sick and injured people were transported by horse and cart. That changed in September 1914, when the British Red Cross introduced the first-ever motorised ambulance.

The Scottish Women's Hospitals followed suit. Their vehicles were donated by their supporters and were essentially the same as those used by the Red Cross – except that they had the Scottish Women's Hospitals livery painted on them.

Scottish Women's Hospitals ambulances included space for several stretcher cases, and some had springs upon which the stretchers were hung to minimise pain and discomfort for patients travelling on bumpy roads.

Several different makes of motor car and lorry were used by medical units on the front lines. The popular American Model-T Ford car was often converted for use as an ambulance.

Flight of the Black Cat

Captain Ian Henderson leaned over the side of his open-topped cockpit and craned his neck, scanning the sky above and below him. The wind blasted his cheeks, the noise of the engine and propeller roared in his ears.

Far beneath the wings of his single-seat biplane, through gaps in the ragged, dense blankets of grey cloud, he could see the bomb-blasted fields and shattered buildings of farming villages. Above, cold and mysterious, were the infinite Heavens.

'Where are you hiding, Bosche?' Henderson said to himself, cursing his German foe as he sat back down in the relatively quiet cocoon of his cockpit.

He pulled off his leather-bound goggles for a moment. His eyes smarted in the rushing air as he wiped the sweat and engine oil from his brow. He checked the ammunition in his well-worn machine guns and scanned his instruments.

The young pilot was something of a rising star in the Royal Flying Corps, notching up a series of successes against the fighter aircraft of the German Luftstreitkräfte. Now it was time to add to that total. He knew the enemy was out there somewhere, so he throttled up the 200-horsepower engine and got ready for action.

It was then that his propeller came off.

At first, just for a moment, it was as though nothing had happened. But the tell-tale change in the tone of the engine made Henderson realise he was in serious trouble. He could also sense it through the controls.

Suddenly he felt his stomach lurch, as the plane began to drop through the air. He gripped the controls tighter and tried to level off, but the aircraft was already nosing into a dive.

The dials on the dashboard span and jerked. The altimeter revealed that he would hit the ground very hard, very soon, unless he could find a way to regain control.

The plane rattled and shook as the descent began taking its toll. Henderson knew of pilots who had met their doom when the stress of a steep dive caused their wings to come off. Having no propeller was deadly enough without that added challenge. He used all his strength to pull, push and lever the controls, desperately trying to find a friendly current of air to ride on.

Still the aircraft kept plunging.

Buildings and hedgerows became sharper and more detailed as the ground loomed closer. Somehow, he just managed to lift the aircraft's nose to make the descent less steep. The plane leapt from side to side as he wrestled with the controls for the rudder and the wing-mounted ailerons, trying to steer to an open patch where he might be able to set down without slamming into a wall or a ditch.

By now he was level with the tops of the trees. In just a few seconds he would strike the ground. His pulse throbbed in his chest and temples. He had to force himself to remain calm, not to allow his tense muscles and sweaty fingers to yank too hard on the controls.

Sensing he was only inches away from the soil, Henderson closed his eyes.

THUD! CRASH! BATTER!

The plane smashed into the ground, wrecking the undercarriage and damaging the propeller-less nose and its huge, square radiator. The fuselage skidded along the ground and the wings shook violently.

Eventually the aircraft jerked to a halt and the engine spluttered, then died. Smoke and steam poured from the wreckage.

A few moments passed. There was no sign of life.

Then a leather-gloved hand emerged and gripped the lip of the cockpit. There was a groan.

Henderson checked his legs and arms, wiggled his fingers and toes. 'Still in one piece,' he reassured himself and leaned his head back, his smile a crescent of ivory white against his smoke-blackened face.

He coughed and came to his senses. There was no time to relax. He had to get out in case the fuel tank caught fire.

Gripping the fuselage he began to haul himself up, then paused for a moment. He grabbed his map and tucked it under his arm, then reached out to an object tied to the dashboard – the toy black cat his sister Angela had given him.

'How many more lives does this leave us with, then?' said Henderson to his mascot as he pulled it free, then climbed out of the wreck and staggered away.

Soon he was back among his friends in the squadron, rested and recovered, with another exciting tale to tell – and ready to fly and fight another day. Yet, returning to earth with a bump was a reminder of how far Henderson had come since the war began. In many ways it was amazing that he had survived this long.

Henderson's wartime adventure had begun quietly and unpromisingly with a miserably cold, long winter in the army reserves, far from the high life of the Royal Flying Corps.

He was given a job guarding the army's big weapons arsenal at Woolwich in London. His accommodation was a stuffy little hole where he and the other men lived on a diet of tinned beef.

Henderson, who had been trained as an officer, was in charge of the sentries who patrolled the premises, and he had to check regularly that they were guarding the place properly. It wasn't a job he enjoyed.

One night, while out checking on the men, Henderson and his orderly were caught in a storm. They were walking along a riverbank and a gust of wind sent the orderly reeling, blowing him into the water. Instinctively, Henderson jumped in and managed to drag the man out.

The storm had pulled down trees and it started to snow. Exhausted and frozen, the pair became disoriented and ended up stumbling through a ditch full of dirty water. As they returned to base they were almost shot by one of their own men. It was very late and they were soaked to the skin.

To make matters worse, the stove had gone out in Henderson's room and the window above his bed had blown open – his mattress was sodden.

So when Henderson was finally sent across the English Channel to fight on the front line, it was a relief at first to leave behind such miserable conditions. But he quickly realised there were certain advantages to being on the home front – like not being shot to pieces.

By the late spring of 1915, he was right in the thick of the action with the Argyll and Sutherland Highlanders. The Germans were trying to take the Belgian town of Ypres and the Argylls, together with other British regiments, were trying to stop them.

To get to Ypres, Henderson and his company marched along roads jammed with military and civilian traffic. There were horse-drawn artillery carriages, wounded troops, ambulance wagons, transport wagons, motor cars of all shapes and sizes, dispatch riders on motorcycles, riders on horseback, people on pedal bicycles ringing their bells furiously, and a constant chatter of French and English.

As they got nearer the front line the chaos and signs of battle intensified. They had to walk across open fields strewn with the dead bodies of men and horses. When they finally arrived, they found the city of Ypres in ruins.

Henderson was posted to a front-line trench near the ruined city. The network of trenches went on for miles and miles, and his was just one tiny part of it. The Germans were dug in nearby on the other side of a small hill and Henderson rarely saw them. But their shells continually blasted and pounded the Argylls, and the number of dead and wounded began to mount.

The trench was cramped and freezing cold, especially after dark. When it rained, the muddy floor became a quagmire. Henderson cursed himself for forgetting his coat.

Eventually he found an old coat probably left by a wounded soldier. He found an old sack, too, and put that around his shoulders over the coat. They were already sodden but they were better than nothing.

The rain continued. Hour after hour. Henderson's boots became like big mud pies, and his legs and kilt were caked with the stuff. At night he huddled in a dugout in the wall of the trench. The dugout was so small that his knees stuck out into the rain.

Days and nights were spent like this and Henderson began to think he might have been better off back at the ammo dump in London after all. To try to stave off madness, he would let his imagination paint a new picture of his surroundings. His smelly dugout became an alcove in a nice restaurant, where he was served a fine meal at a grand table with a white tablecloth, glasses and cutlery.

Letters from home – his parents and wee sister Angela – were what really kept him going. Angela sounded very grown up these days and she gave him advice on how to fend off bombs, which made him smile. Henderson was delighted by the drawings that accompanied her letters.

As a result of the shellfire and snipers' bullets, many of Henderson's comrades were killed. Those who survived did their best to keep their spirits up. It was not uncommon to hear survivors of a shell attack singing or humming the haunting Scottish lament 'The Flowers of the Forest' as they went about their business.

Eventually Henderson's company was relieved. The men were sent back from the trenches for a few days' rest at their billet, about a mile or so behind the lines. 'Thank God,' muttered Henderson, stamping the caked-on mud from his boots as he marched along the road.

Early one morning, Henderson woke up with a fright. The relative peace of the billet had been shattered by a terrific sound. German artillery shells were exploding everywhere. He rushed outside and took cover, then looked around, trying to work out what was happening.

The billet was a farm building on the edge of an open field. A road passed through the middle of the field leading toward the woods, from which huge columns of black smoke were rising. After a while the smoke became so dense Henderson could hardly see the trees.

Just beyond the woods, and out of sight, Henderson knew there were more front-line trenches containing his fellow soldiers – he presumed they were now the focus of the German shellfire.

Soon rag-tag bunches of wounded men emerged from the woods and began making their way slowly down the road toward the billet, stumbling along and helping each other as best they could. The shells seemed to follow them, blasting craters in the ground with monstrous force. Henderson looked on in horror as two little groups of the retreating men were hit, their bodies torn apart.

A company was ordered to leave the billet and reinforce the trenches. Henderson watched them go, as the shells continued to fall. The men had no choice but to cross the field via the road to reach the cover of the woods. But before they had even gone ten yards they had five casualties – three men blown to bits when a shell slammed into the ground, and two wounded.

When the survivors reached the edge of the woods, they were met by a new wave of terror-stricken men running in the opposite direction, shouting, 'Gas! Everybody has been killed by gas! The trenches are taken! The Germans are in the woods!'

One of the officers took control of the situation and tried to calm everything down. The retreating men were turned around and all the troops marched towards the trenches together, rifles and bayonets at the ready in case the Germans really had advanced as far as the woods.

Then it was Henderson's turn to go.

'I want you to follow them and join the counter-attack,' ordered a senior officer.

'Yes, sir!' replied Henderson.

His company set off and made it through the woods without casualties.

They soon discovered that the Germans had only taken a few trenches, so the counter-attack was called off for the time being. Henderson's platoon rested for the night in a ditch near a chateau – a large French country house.

They were woken up at two in the morning with orders to make a shelter in the kitchen garden of the chateau.

'Why couldn't we have a bit more rest?' said a young soldier about Henderson's age.

'Bosche will start shelling us as soon as he's had breakfast,' replied Henderson. 'If we don't get this shelter dug out before then, we'll be done for.'

In response, the soldier began digging frantically in the dark, uprooting the flowers and vegetables.

Just as Henderson had predicted, around nine o'clock in the morning the firing began. A shell came hurtling straight towards the half-finished dugout where he was crouched. It whooshed and rumbled through the air, and when it hit the ground it exploded with a deafening *BOOM!*

Henderson wiped the spattered mud from his face and tried to clear his stinging eyes of the white smoke that had enveloped him. He turned to his left, and then his right. The three men next to him were dead. Somehow, by the grace of God, he was untouched.

It was obvious the shellfire wasn't just random luck – the German guns must have located the British troops' position. If Henderson and his comrades stayed there, they would all end up dead. Hastily they made a plan before breaking cover.

While half the men went to try to re-take some trenches, Henderson took charge of the other half, who would wait in reserve until ordered to attack.

'We're going to take cover a few hundred yards up the road that runs past the chateau – follow me!' Henderson commanded his men.

In double time they trooped up the road and hid behind a hedge.

'Corporal!' shouted Henderson.

'Sir!' came the reply.

'Get these men back to the dressing station for first aid.' He nodded in the direction of two soldiers with shrapnel wounds.

'Yes, sir!' With the help of two able-bodied men, the corporal quickly went off with the wounded.

'Now, listen up, the rest of you,' continued Henderson. 'We're going to . . .'

He was cut off by a new sound coming from above.

'Damn it – a Hun aeroplane!' cursed Henderson. 'Keep your heads down!'

The observer in the aircraft must have spotted the kilted soldiers below, as Henderson clearly saw him sending a signal back to his artillery. It wouldn't be long before the German gunners started hammering them again.

'Let's keep moving!' Henderson commanded.

He led his men further down the road to a ditch that gave them a little cover when they lay on their bellies and stretched themselves flat out. As they did so the hedge they'd been sheltering behind was directly hit by four shells and blasted to atoms. Once again, Henderson knew they had to move on.

Next to a stone gateway he found a large shell hole, better shelter for his men than a ditch.

But he soon discovered that the gateway was being used as a target by the German gunners. A light field gun was shooting at it with small shells that made a *whizz-bang* sound, like fireworks. They flew past Henderson's head as he clambered down into the hole. He and his men hunkered down and waited for the shelling to stop.

Later, once they were fairly sure the Germans had given up shelling for the time being, they went to re-take a couple of trenches only to find that they had already been taken by the British side during an earlier counter-attack.

After that things went quiet until early the following morning when Henderson and the others watched German soldiers creeping through the woods in ones and twos. Another British regiment – the Glosters – led a counter-attack and the Argylls joined in. The Germans scarpered.

When Henderson got out of the wood again, he looked up. He kept thinking about the German aeroplane that had spotted him and his men. He was fed up of being on the ground at the mercy of aerial attacks, and wished he could fly up there and knock those planes out of the sky.

Upon his return from the front line, he found a visitor waiting. 'Dad!' he shouted and rushed to his father, who gripped him in a bear hug.

Henderson's father, Sir David Henderson, was a senior figure in the British forces. Like his son, he had served in the Argyll and

Sutherland Highlanders, and was highly decorated for his part in wars fought long ago.

He was now one of the leaders of the Royal Flying Corps – the British air force – and a skilled pilot himself.

'How are you, laddie?' asked Sir David in his Glaswegian brogue. Soon the pair were deep in conversation, the younger man retelling the exploits of the last few days like the veteran he already was, while the older man nodded his approval. But in spite of the bravado, it was obvious that Ian was troubled.

'I'm desperate to get out, Dad,' admitted Henderson at last.

'Really? A man could get himself shot for deserter's talk like that,' replied his father with mock seriousness.

'You know what I mean,' replied Henderson. 'We were spotted by a flying Hun, who relayed our position to their guns. We were nearly done for. It was beastly.' He sighed. 'I want to be up there,' he continued, nodding at the sky, 'doing something about it.'

'I know,' said his father, his dark eyes glowing as he grinned under his thick moustache. 'That's why I'm here. Get your stuff together – you're about to join the Royal Flying Corps.'

'But . . .?' Henderson couldn't believe what he was hearing.

'Don't worry, it's all been arranged, laddie,' said his father, holding out his hands in a calming gesture. 'It's what you always wanted, is it not?'

'Yes, but . . .'

'No more buts,' said Sir David. 'Your company can look after themselves, and you'll have plenty of opportunity to catch up with them from time to time. The best thing you can do now is get airborne and help them by taking the fight to the Kaiser's men in the sky.'

For years, Henderson had dreamed of learning to fly like his father, and since the start of the war he had yearned to join the ranks of the RFC. Now that it was actually happening, and after all he had been through in the trenches of the army's ground war during the past few weeks, it seemed a bit unreal to be suddenly plucked out of the mud and sent into the sky.

He soon forgot his reservations once he put on the RFC uniform and took to the air. Flying was simply wonderful. It was in his blood.

No more muddy trenches, no more shells ringing in his ears or corpses strewn about. The Royal Flying Corps offered freedom from all that. High above the ground, on a clear day, he could see the Earth curving away into the distance.

His career as a pilot began at the Central Flying School near Stonehenge on Salisbury Plain. He flew a Henri Farman, almost identical to the Boxkite aircraft his father had learned to fly on.

Indeed the Farman, like the Boxkite, was more like a huge kite than a plane. It had long landing skids sticking out from the front like horns. It was not a great machine, but for Henderson it was a thrill just to be at the controls and learning how to fly up and away.

Learning how to land was even more important. After the Henri Farman, Henderson was given a Royal Aircraft Factory BE2a, which was much better to fly, but he found it a beast to land.

Henderson was taught how to drop bombs with the BE2a. They were mounted on racks under the wings. When a cable was pulled in the cockpit, the bombs were released. It was important to be very sure the whole lot was dropped. Landing a BE2a was bumpy enough without a bomb hanging off the wing.

After several weeks' training, the instructors decided Henderson was ready and sent him to France. This was it – active service. As he travelled to join his squadron he wondered how long it would be before he faced a Hun – or a Bosche, to give the Germans their other wartime nickname – in air-to-air combat.

Henderson's squadron was based at Hesdigneul, near the French port town of Calais and the border with Belgium, from where the Germans were attacking.

It was now December 1915 and the weather was hopeless. It rained and rained until the aerodrome was a great mass of mud and water. The aircraft often got bogged down before the pilots could reach take-off speed, especially if there were two men on board. For a good while Henderson didn't get airborne at all.

At least he had a comfortable billet – a room in a huge chateau eleven miles from the front line. They could hardly hear the guns at all from there. And Henderson found the people around him very pleasant.

He spent his time getting to know the mechanics, who did a difficult and dangerous job at all hours of the day and night, often in foul weather, to keep the aircraft in good working order. These men tended to be the unsung heroes of the flying corps, but Henderson quickly realised that the air crews absolutely depended on them.

The waiting was tedious. One evening, a concert was held and, as his contribution to the programme, Henderson sang the tongue-twister 'Sister Susie's Sewing Shirts for Soldiers'. It went down a storm with the other men and the concerts became a regular part of camp life. The squadron set up a cinema projector, too, so they could watch 'movies'.

The new year came in and the weather remained dreadful. But

the aircrews couldn't stay on the ground for ever. Eventually, very early one morning, Henderson managed to take off on a reconnaissance mission.

Accompanied by an observer, Henderson flew over the front lines to see what the Germans were up to and to find out how effective the British manoeuvres had been. Things got even more exciting when the Germans began firing up at his plane. Henderson felt quite proud that the enemy considered him such a threat, going to all that trouble to try to bring him down. But they didn't get near him.

On long winter flights such as this Henderson thanked God for his mother and all the clothes she'd sent him. There was a scarf, gloves, a leather flying cap and big snow boots – all fur-lined to help stave off the deadly high-altitude cold. Henderson's mother had also sent him a long thick coat to replace the filthy second-hand one he'd found in the trenches.

Not only did the new coat help save him from freezing to death in the cockpit, it had other protective powers too.

While flying through German shellfire something pinged sharply against Henderson's arm.

'Was that you?' he shouted to his observer.

'What?' the observer shouted back.

'Did you chuck something at me?'

'No! But don't tempt me – you need to stop mucking about and get us out of here!' The observer laughed, and Henderson did too.

It was only when they landed that Henderson realised he had been hit by a piece of shell, about the size of a pea. It had torn a hole in his new coat. Thanks to the thick double-lining, it hadn't pierced his skin.

Soon they were back in the sky, where Henderson engaged with a German aircraft for the first time. It was a Fokker Eindecker. These machines had single wings, so were not biplanes like the RFC aircraft. When Henderson spotted the Eindecker, he and his observer were so excited they dived at him and gave chase with great speed.

Henderson couldn't help being impressed by the Eindecker, with its grey fuselage and huge German emblem – the Iron Cross – painted upon its wings and tail. It carried a clever new innovation – a synchronised machine gun up front so its pilot could shoot through his propeller.

The Eindecker was also sprightly. Since Henderson had orders not to follow an enemy aircraft over its lines, he had to let it go. But the thrill of having chased away their first enemy aircraft put the two RFC fliers in high spirits. They began to sing.

Singing soon became part of the routine of flying, and Henderson and his observer liked to sing as often as possible during a flight. Even at the top of their voices it was difficult to hear anything over the din of the plane. But when Henderson performed a controlled shut-down of the engine for a brief time, they would keep singing – ecstatic at the sound of their harmonies floating over the clouds.

They had an audience, too – Henderson's Black Cat, his present from Angela. The toy cat was attached above the dashboard at the start of each flight and it appeared to jiggle its arms throughout.

The only time Henderson couldn't see Black Cat was when he needed to get a map out during a reconnaissance mission. The maps were large and filled the cockpit when he rolled them out to check his route. Once they were neatly stowed, Black Cat would be back in view.

Besides maps, there was sophisticated kit on board the RFC aircraft.

A wireless radio was used to direct gunners on the ground to the right targets. On one occasion Henderson saw a flash coming from a big house. After careful thought and a good look at it, he decided it must be a German gun firing.

He wirelessed the enemy position to his own guns on the ground. To his great satisfaction, after a few shots, the house went up in a cloud of brick dust and smoke. Henderson gleefully signalled 'Hit!'

Of course Henderson did his own firing, too. One evening he and his observer were coming back from a reconnaissance flight over the German line when their singing was cut short.

'Three Huns coming our way!' shouted the observer.

'Yes, obviously returning from a mission over our lines!' replied Henderson.

The incoming German aircraft were flying at a higher altitude than Henderson's plane.

'I expect they're going to dive and give it to us hot!' shouted the observer.

However, the Germans appeared to take no notice of them, so concerned were they with making their escape. Henderson did not like being ignored.

'I'm going to increase altitude, then we'll give it to them with both guns!' shouted Henderson

'Righto!' came the reply, and the observer began aiming his machine gun.

Once Henderson got as close as he dared, he lined up his own gun. 'Fire!' he shouted.

RAT-TAT-TAT! RAT-TAT-TAT! went the machine guns.

'Wait, what's going on ...!' shouted Henderson, as bullets began ripping at his plane from below. He broke off from firing and directed his goggled eyes down at the ground.

Some French anti-aircraft gunners had spotted the planes overhead and opened fire.

The French gunners were Henderson's allies and were obviously aiming at the aircraft bearing the Iron Cross. But as rotten luck would have it they hit the very thing they wanted to avoid – Henderson's plane.

The Germans flew away while a frustrated Henderson limped back to the aerodrome with a hole in his tail the size of a football. Not all the crews had been as fortunate.

Later that day, the Germans dropped a note on the aerodrome. It was about some missing men from Henderson's squadron.

The note said they had landed behind German lines with engine trouble. They had been taken prisoner but were all right. This was the civilised, gentlemanly side of war, thought Henderson. Unlike some of his ongoing training with the Royal Flying Corps.

The RFC had devised fiendish and sometimes bizarre ways of toughening men up. After dinner one evening Henderson was strapped to a chair and blindfolded for an 'Archying'. This exercise was meant to improve a pilot's capacity to cope with being hit by shrapnel from an anti-aircraft gun, or 'Archy'.

Tangerines and other pieces of fruit – the 'shrapnel' – were hurled at Henderson's face and body for an extended period of time. Throughout it all he was expected to keep a stiff upper lip. This he did, and then went to bed.

Henderson ended up spending a lot more time in bed that spring. A nasty infection got into his lungs and he was struck down with pleurisy. Out of action for weeks, he couldn't wait to get back up in the air.

Luckily he recovered enough to take part in a major confrontation which began that summer between the Allies and the Germans on the ground. It became known as the Battle of the Somme and was a turning point in the First World War.

Henderson escorted a group of five bombers over the German lines. While the other aircraft were dropping their bombs, he found himself under attack by an enemy plane. There was quite a tussle, but eventually he shook the marauder off. When he flew off to rejoin his own group, they had completely disappeared.

Henderson could see a big storm coming in from the direction of the British lines on a strong west wind. He would have to fly through the storm to get home.

On the way he met German planes coming in the opposite direction, a group of ten or so, and he had a brief dogfight with one or two of them. But they scuttled home before the advancing tempest. Henderson wasn't so fortunate.

He was still just inside the German lines when he flew into the thundering cloud. It was pitch black and he couldn't see a thing. He dropped down several hundred feet to try to get under the cloud but flew into a terrific hail shower.

When he tried to stick his head out of the cockpit for a better look, the hailstones cut his skin to pieces. In the end he managed to cross the British lines and land safely. But there was no sign of the five bombers he had been escorting. They must have lost their way in the storm, a sobering reminder of the dangerous conditions in which they were all operating.

But Henderson was determined to carry on. Soon he set off on another bombing raid, this time as the lead bomber, with a big flag on his tail. Their target was about fifteen miles beyond the German lines. They dropped their bombs as planned and everything went beautifully until they were halfway back.

Looking over his shoulder, Henderson saw that one of his group was surrounded by German aircraft, who were all firing at the poor fellow. He was trapped, just circling round and round helplessly – it transpired later that the pilot's gun had jammed. Seeing his comrade in serious trouble, Henderson banked his own aircraft into a sharp turn and went back to give him a bit of help.

He flew towards the attackers. They were all so busy terrorising the isolated British plane that they didn't notice him approaching. He gained height steadily until he was directly above one of them. Then he launched into a terrific dive, firing ferociously.

Down he went, closer and closer. He came so close that he could see the German observer trying to lock his machine gun onto him. But Henderson kept on firing until suddenly the observer slumped lifeless over the side of his machine, his arms dangling.

The pilot must have been hit too, because the plane suddenly dived absolutely vertically. One of Henderson's comrades later said he saw him go into a spinning nosedive, but Henderson didn't stick around to watch.

By now all the other German aircraft were above him and he was afraid they would turn nasty. Luckily they seemed to be so rattled by what had just happened that they flew off, leaving Henderson and the other planes to return home and land safely.

Returning home in one piece was something that could never be taken for granted. Henderson was reminded of this when his squadron was paid a visit by a battalion of Argylls. It was good to see one or two faces he recognised from his old regiment. But there were many men missing. They had had a bad time of it in the trenches of late, with fourteen officers lost.

The RFC had suffered heavy losses, too. When Henderson's group had come out to the Somme just five weeks earlier, there were twenty pilots. Now only six out of that original twenty were left. The rest were either wounded, missing or dead.

These missions were the most dangerous so far. Most of their days were spent flying twenty or thirty miles behind German lines. They bombed the enemy's aerodromes, ammunition dumps, railways, troops – everything that might possibly undermine the enemy's military operation. Then they had to try to get home alive.

Airmen needed to look out for each other if they were going to survive. This fact was brought home to Henderson while on a bombing raid led by Captain Williams, a fellow pilot.

Williams had attached long streamers to his plane to mark him out as the leader. The only trouble with such flags and streamers was that they made an aircraft a lot more visible to the enemy too.

A German spotted Williams early on and went straight in for the kill. Henderson was flying above Williams at a height of more than 3,000 metres and could see the dogfight taking place right down in front of him.

Williams seemed to have been wounded by the first shot or so because his plane went down at once, more or less out of control. The German raced after him.

Watching both planes turn in circles as they descended, Henderson flew after the German, firing when he could, although he was afraid of hitting Williams, who was underneath.

Williams flew into a cloud at just over 1,200 metres, followed by his pursuer with guns blazing, who in turn was being followed and fired at by Henderson.

In the cloud Henderson lost them both. He emerged at 1,000 metres and couldn't see either Williams or the German aircraft anywhere. Then he spotted five more Huns underneath him. Deciding to attack before he was attacked, he dived on the last one, who dived to avoid him and then flew away.

Henderson was now down to 600 metres, flying above the German trenches. At that level his plane would soon be vulnerable to fire from the ground, so he pulled away as sharply as he could over his own side's trenches to the aerodrome and landed.

Williams's plane had made it home but was smashed and snapped and covered with holes. When Henderson peered inside, he could see the seat and rudder pedals were soaked in blood.

When he found Williams, he was alive and being bandaged up.

'I managed to regain control while in the cloud and shook off the Hun,' said Williams with an exhausted smile. 'You saved my life, Ian,' he continued. 'If you hadn't gone after him, he would have done for me.'

'It was nothing,' said Henderson, feeling a little embarrassed. 'You would have done the same for me.'

There then came a turning point in the whole campaign.

After lunch on 14 September, the squadron was addressed by a colleague of Henderson's father, General Trenchard, Chief of the Air Staff. He told them that the British were going to try to strike a decisive blow against the Germans, to help bring the war to an end once and for all, and to do so they were going to unleash a mighty new weapon.

That night British bombers from every aerodrome in the Somme area were sent out with orders to hit anything and everything belonging to the enemy. The aim was to leave the Germans broken and in shock. Then, early the next morning, a big ground assault began.

Henderson was sent up on 'contact patrol'. This meant flying low over the German lines in a single-seat BE12 machine to find out how far the British advance was getting.

Henderson found the view fascinating. He could see British soldiers running forward and jumping into the German trenches, then running after the retreating enemy.

His aircraft got shot up by Archies and machine-gunners, and he was nearly hit by his own side's shells. But all that training with fruit paid off and he hung on grimly until the job was done.

By the time he got back his face was black with engine oil, but he was bursting with excitement at being able to report on the ground troops' advance.

Later that day he went up again, and it was then that he saw the new weapon General Trenchard had told them about. It was the most wonderful invention he had ever seen – the tank!

These huge, diamond-shaped metal beasts were heavily armoured, with toothed caterpillar tracks on their wheels and cannons protruding from either side. They knocked down trees left and right as they went, and smashed through enemy trenches.

He was so busy observing the tanks forcing their way behind enemy lines that Henderson and his plane took a battering from the Archies. Wires and struts were shot at and his engine was hit again, but he was determined not to return to base until he'd seen one of the tanks, swiftly followed by a column of British soldiers, capture a village. They cheered and waved at Henderson as he flew over.

It was quite amazing to see how an armoured tank was able to lead and shield an advance by a group of soldiers against the enemy artillery. Perhaps the stalemate of both sides being stuck in trenches and endlessly hammered by each other's shells could now be broken. And if the British side had the tanks, then it made victory over the Germans a bit more likely.

But the enemy was very far from being beaten. Henderson was reminded of this while flying over a village – or what had once been a village, it was now in ruins – when terrific machine-gun fire opened on him. His aircraft was hammered so badly the engine nearly stopped. He struggled back to the nearest friendly aerodrome and telephoned in his report.

Henderson flew close to disaster so many times that he felt he must have at least nine lives. Perhaps Angela's Black Cat is looking out for me, he thought.

Many pilots were not so lucky. Henderson was leading a patrol over enemy lines when they were attacked by two big German planes. They went for Henderson at first, but he shot at them fiercely and they turned their firepower on the two aircraft behind him instead.

Before Henderson had time to turn around and help he saw one of his own patrol catch fire and go down blazing. The pilot in the other RFC plane must have been shot dead because he went down too, in a spin, and fell to pieces.

It was a sickening sight. Henderson felt sure his turn would be next, but he must somehow have frightened the Germans. They didn't attack him again and instead flew off.

As winter approached some of the squadron were given new aeroplanes. Henderson was among the lucky ones. The new aircraft was a SPAD, and Henderson thought it was the most wonderful machine imaginable. Fast, strong and agile, it could even be driven at 130mph along the ground.

Henderson was then moved to the elite 56 Squadron, which spent a lot of time based back across the English Channel defending Britain against enemy air raids. Under cover of darkness the German airforce had begun dropping bombs on cities such as Edinburgh and London using Zeppelins – airships whose crew could roam about in large, comfortable cabins slung underneath gigantic cigar-shaped balloons filled with hydrogen and driven by propellers.

As the war went on, the airmen of 56 Squadron faced a foe that was even faster, stronger and more versatile than the Zeppelins. This was the Grosskampfflugzeug – or Gotha – a large and elegant twin-engined bomber aeroplane with a three-man crew, sent in formations of twenty or more to attack British cities during the day.

The Gothas carried up to half a ton – 500kg – of bombs in their fuselage and, propelled by two 260-horsepower Mercedes engines on their wings, could easily fly at a height of more than 3,300 metres. The Gothas brought terror, death and destruction to the home front, while the RFC squadrons did their best to limit the damage.

Henderson's father was in charge of defending the homeland from such attacks, and he was heavily criticised for not doing enough. But it was an impossible situation.

There were not enough men and aircraft to prevent all the Gothas and Zeppelins getting through – plus Britain's air defences were too disorganised. Henderson's father began arguing for the creation of a new and improved Royal Air Force. Meanwhile, in their letters and occasional meetings, Henderson comforted his father as best he could.

There was still a war to be won on mainland Europe, however, and while he participated in home defence Henderson was never very far from the thick of the action in the skies over France, constantly pushing himself and his aircraft to the limit. His most successful month was July 1917 – but it could easily have been his last.

He was credited with shooting down four Albatross DVs that month. It took his confirmed tally up to seven – but there was evidence he had actually shot down more enemy planes than that. Henderson felt excited and optimistic. They were really going at the Huns now.

But there were still emergencies to overcome, including the mission during which Henderson's propeller came off in mid-air. The controls jammed and he went into a dive. He managed to crash-land but the machine was wrecked. Somehow he walked away with barely a scratch. The lucky Black Cat was still watching over him and he made sure that he salvaged it from the wreckage.

Henderson held his own in a squadron that was filled with the best of the best – Arthur Rhys-Davids, James McCudden, Albert Ball, Cecil Lewis, to give a few famous names. The friendship between the men was wonderful. Despite the dangers they faced every time they took to the skies, they joked, they sang, there was poetry – and some great concerts, too.

When Henderson was granted leave of absence or posted on home defence, he would join the 'chaps' for some sport or other, or take someone out for a spin on his motorcycle. And then there were the girls, of course.

A dance was organised when the squadron was back in 'Blighty' – a favourite nickname for Britain – for home defence.

They were based at Bekesbourne Aerodrome near Canterbury, halfway between London and the English Channel.

The weather was cloudless and perfect for bombing, but there was no sign of any Zeppelins or Gothas so the men kept busy with their dance preparations. They went to Canterbury to round up some eager young ladies and brought them back to the aerodrome, where they had put up a marquee with a dancefloor made from some planking a senior officer had scrounged from somewhere.

On the night of the dance the marquee looked wonderful. The tables were beautifully laid with fine china and silver, which twinkled in the candle light. The open ends of the tent flapped in the gentle breeze of the fine summer's night.

Henderson and the others popped champagne corks while the girls, dressed in their evening gowns, were invited to stand in the long grass on the edge of the aerodrome. Henderson and his friend Cecil Lewis then jumped in a couple of aircraft and gave an exhibition of stunt flying.

'That was wonderful, Captain Henderson,' said a pretty young lady after Henderson and Lewis had rejoined the crowd.

'Oh, it was nothing,' Henderson replied, smiling bashfully.

They all ate a beautiful dinner prepared by the squadron cooks and afterwards Henderson led the singing while someone played the fiddle. The evening was full of laughter, talking and dancing.

These were happy times, despite the worries of war. On another happy occasion a photograph was taken showing Henderson, grinning like the Cheshire cat, looking dapper in a blazer with his black hair slicked back and two pretty young ladies standing next to him.

Perhaps one of these girls might have hoped that the dashing young pilot would one day become her husband. Who would this hero of the skies choose as a wife with whom to start a family? He could have taken his pick.

But Henderson's story was to have a rather different ending.

In the spring of 1918 he was sent to Scotland, to the training school at Turnberry on the Ayrshire coast. He wrote to tell his father, who was pleased to know he would be in a part of the country that was home to many of the family's relatives and ancestors.

The training school was an opportunity to test different machines and weapons, and to learn new techniques before rejoining the fray. It was a busy but relaxing period for Henderson. When he had some time off, he loved to ride his motorcycle, and he and the others sometimes took an old motorboat out along the coast.

His father wrote to tell him that he had resigned from his top job in the air force, as he felt he had done as much as he could do and wanted to try something different. 'I would like to come up to see you, my lad,' he wrote, 'but it is rather a long journey.'

Henderson wrote back to comfort his father, for he knew running and reorganising the air force had been an exhausting job. He described his training at Turnberry, and the exciting new aircraft and weapons he was testing. 'I'm looking forward to telling you more about it when I get leave to visit home,' he added.

Then his letters suddenly stopped.

Instead, on the afternoon of 21 June 1918, Sir David received a telegram:

*** Deeply regret [to] inform you Captain Ian Henry David Henderson killed near here in aeroplane accident this forenoon. *** Cause of accident unknown. *** Captain Henderson was testing gun as passenger. *** Please wire wishes

RE: FUNERAL WHETHER BODY TO BE SENT HOME OR
BURIAL ARRANGED HERE. *** ACCIDENTS COMMITTEE
ASKED TO INVESTIGATE. ***

Henderson's flying companion that day had been another experienced pilot and friend called Harold Redler. Henderson had piloted the plane – a De Havilland – when it took off.

Then, as they had been trained to do, they carefully swapped places in mid-air, by climbing over the fuselage and holding tight to the wing frames, so that Redler could fly while Henderson tested the gun. They flew at high speed and very low altitude through the neck of a gulley as it opened out to the sea.

It was then that things went horribly wrong. Just as the aircraft went into a climbing turn, the wind suddenly whipped it viciously and Redler lost control. The De Havilland slammed into the ground, left wing down, and both men were killed.

Two young men who had survived for months in the intense heat of battle over the front line in France and in the war-torn skies above Britain had been taken out by a freak gust of wind at home during a straightforward training exercise. In that instant, Captain Ian Henderson joined the ranks of the many young RFC aces – several of them his friends – who would not live to see the end of the First World War.

The luck of Black Cat had finally run out. All that was left for the Henderson family to remember their son was a gravestone in Ayrshire, some scraps of correspondence, a few photographs and other personal effects. Plus the rich but fading memories of shared conversations, close embraces, gestures and companionable silences – all testimony to a heroic life spent soaring above the clouds.

WAR REPORT

Personnel: Captain Ian Henderson was born in 1896 into a wealthy Scottish family. His father was a Glaswegian ship-builder's son called Sir David Henderson. Sir David was a highly decorated soldier and pioneering military pilot who became a founder of the Royal Flying Corps in 1912. Henderson's mother, Henrietta Dundas, belonged to an aristocratic Edinburgh family.

Henderson grew up with a younger sister, Angela. He was given an elite school education in England at Eton College and then Sandhurst military college, after which he joined his father's Scottish regiment – the Argyll and Sutherland Highlanders – rising to the rank of Captain.

After war broke out Henderson was sent to fight on the front line but was transferred to the RFC to train as a pilot in the summer of 1915 and served in No. 2, No. 19 and No. 56 Squadrons.

Henderson was officially credited with seven aerial-combat victories and was awarded the Military Cross for gallantry during operations against the enemy. He was sent for further training in Scotland in the spring of 1918 but was killed in a flying accident at Turnberry on the Ayrshire coast on 21 June.

He was buried in nearby Girvan at Doune Cemetery. His name is inscribed, along with other flying-school members who lost their lives, on a tall granite memorial on Turnberry golf course. He was twenty-one years old when he died.

The loss devastated Sir David, who devoted the rest of his career to humanitarian work, including running the International League of Red Cross Societies in Geneva, Switzerland. He was also a strong supporter of the creation of the Scottish National

War Memorial in Edinburgh Castle, which commemorates the nation's war dead. Sir David died in 1921 aged 59.

The Henderson family paid a high price for Sir David and Ian's love of flying. But the two men left behind the legacy of a new and improved Royal Air Force. Plans for it had been drawn up by Sir David and were implemented in 1917. As a result Sir David Henderson was considered by Sir Hugh Trenchard, Chief of the Air Staff, to be the true founding father of the RAF.

Event Log: 'The Fokker Scourge' was a term used by British newspapers in 1915 to describe the threat from German aircraft, which were thought to be winning the war in the skies at that time. The air superiority of the Fliegertruppen – the Imperial German Air Force, later known as the Luftstreitkräfte – had to be overturned. That is one reason why young men such as Captain Ian Henderson were plucked from the ground war in the trenches and placed into the cockpits of RFC aircraft to take on the Germans.

The term 'Fokker Scourge' referred mainly to the Fokker Eindecker aircraft, which was a monoplane with a single wing on either side. It was the first aircraft to have a synchronised machine gun that could fire through its propeller straight at its target. RFC aircraft flown by Henderson, such as the BE2 and BE12, were generally outgunned and outmanoeuvred by the Eindecker.

The success of the Eindecker encouraged people to think of all German planes as Fokkers, but another very important German aircraft during the war was a different make – the Albatross D-type. The celebrated German fighter ace Baron Manfred von Richthofen, known as 'the Red Baron', who notched up at least eighty kills, made his reputation in an Albatross DIII. He later flew a Fokker DrI triplane – an aircraft with three wings on top of each other.

Eventually, the Fokker Eindecker met its match when the RFC began using more advanced DH2 and FE2b aircraft, and later even more advanced machines such as Ian Henderson's SE5a.

Inventory: The Royal Aircraft Factory SE5a was a single-seat scout aircraft. Captain Ian Henderson flew this machine in 1917, and shot down several enemy planes from it. The SE5a was faster and more advanced than the aircraft Henderson had flown before, with better cockpit instruments and controls, and a powerful 200-horsepower Hispano-Suiza engine.

The propeller of the SE5a was a tractor, meaning it was mounted in front of a huge H-shaped grille and pulled the aircraft through the air like a tractor pulling a trailer. The SE5a was built by several manufacturers, including Austin Motors, which became a household name after the war as a car manufacturer.

The SE5a had two guns: a .303-inch Vickers machine gun that fired from the nose of the aircraft using a synchronising gear just like a Fokker, so it didn't damage the propeller, and a gas-operated Lewis machine gun on top of the wings that could fire 500 rounds per minute and hit an enemy aircraft from 800 metres away.

The SE5 type was an even better aircraft than the famous Sopwith Camel, and together these two machines helped the RFC and their allies gain air superiority over the German Luftstreitkräfte in 1917 and go on to victory by the end of 1918.

Author's Note

Maps and Activities

Where does the action in this book actually take place? Written descriptions are all very well, but it can be hard to get your head around places you don't know, and events long ago, unless you have a map and some pictures to help.

This is where the internet comes into its own.

You could start by looking up the index of a good old-fashioned printed atlas to find places like 'Turnberry' or 'Jutland'. Turn to the right page and, using the code, find them on the grid. But going online opens up an even wider world of possibilities.

Use an online map service – there are lots to choose from, so get someone to help if you're not sure where to start. By typing in keywords you can look up locations mentioned in this book and learn all sorts of interesting things.

For instance, if you type in the name 'Ypres' – or 'Ieper', its official spelling – then you can pinpoint the location of this city, which was a key First World War battle zone.

Try using the 'get directions' tools to find out how far Ypres is from your own house.

Select 'street view', or similar mode, to see what Ypres looks. like today. Further investigation will reveal the fields where many fallen soldiers are buried, and the Cloth Hall, which was rebuilt after the war.

To avoid confusion, try typing in the name of the country mentioned in the story as well as the village, town or city. For example, 'Loos France'. Hint: Loos is also known as 'Loos-en-Gohelle'.

An online image search of the locations will give you photographs and illustrations, which can help you further in building up a picture of the place.

Most such images will be recent, but using the right keywords will allow you to look for historic images, too – for example, 'Romania 1917' or 'Scottish Women's Hospitals Romania'.

What other places and people from this book can you pinpoint, using online maps and image searches?

Look out for information about exhibitions and activities that may relate to the stories in this book. You could start with the websites of the libraries, museums and archives listed in the next section. Again, a careful keyword search is the easy way to cut to the chase.

Acknowledgements and Further Reading

The real-life stories in this book are based on archival research. Using the key facts of each character's wartime experiences, I've been able to dramatise their stories. Any errors of fact or interpretation here are my responsibility.

I've used a range of sources. These include unpublished diaries, memoirs, letters, records, drawings, diagrams and photographs, as well as published articles, books, records, maps, online archives and museum artefacts.

For 'The Teacher Threw a Bomb', the story of Private George Ramage at Ypres in 1915, the key sources included a multi-volume diary written by Ramage which is kept in the Manuscript Collections of the National Library of Scotland (NLS) in Edinburgh. This story also uses biographical information about Ramage researched by NLS staff.

The regimental diaries of the Gordon Highlanders were also

consulted for Ramage's story and for 'Hell's Orchestra', the story of Private William Wilcock at Loos in 1915. The key source for Wilcock's story is his diary, which is kept at the Gordon Highlanders Museum and Archive in Aberdeen. In addition, the story uses biographical research carried out by archive staff and volunteers.

'Fire in the Sea', the story of Sir Angus Cunninghame-Graham at the Battle of Jutland in 1916, uses sources including a memoir and correspondence kept in the Manuscript Collections of the NLS. This memoir was published in edited form in 1979 by Famedram/Northern Books. Entitled *Random Naval Recollections*, it spans an exciting career of almost fifty years in the navy of which the Battle of Jutland is but one moment.

Other sources used for 'Fire in the Sea' include *The Great Dreadnought: The Strange Story of* HMS *Agincourt, the Mightiest Battleship of World War I* by Richard Hough (Harper & Row, 1967); *British Battleships 1914–1918 (1) The Early Dreadnoughts* by Angus Konstam (Osprey, 2013); and *The Dreadnought Project* at www.dreadnoughtproject.org (2013).

'A Hasty Retreat', the story of Mary Lee Milne, Dr Inglis and the Scottish Women's Hospitals in Romania in 1916, uses sources including the journals of Milne, kept at the NLS Manuscript Collections, as well as the article 'The Dobruja Retreat', published in *Blackwood's Magazine* in 1918. This story also draws upon biographical information researched by staff at the NLS. This story has been radically simplified and the name 'Viktor' given to an unnamed Serbian soldier.

Other sources for 'A Hasty Retreat' include *Dr Elsie Inglis* by Frances Balfour (Doran, 1919); *Elsie Inglis: the woman with the torch* by Eva Shaw McLaren (Macmillan, 1920); *In the service of life: the story of Elsie Inglis and the Scottish Women's Hospitals* by Leah Leneman (Mercat, 1994); and *Between the Lines: Letters and Diaries from Elsie Inglis's Russian Unit* by Audrey Fawcett Cahill (Pentland, 1999).

The key sources for 'Flight of the Black Cat', the story of Captain Ian Henderson of the Argyll and Sutherland Highlanders and Royal Flying Corps, include the private correspondence and papers of Henderson and his immediate family kept at the Archive Collection of the Royal Air Force at Hendon in London. In addition, the classic memoir *Sagittarius Rising* by former RFC pilot Cecil Lewis (Frontline, 2009) contains important references to Ian Henderson, as does *Royal Flying Corps Head Quarters, 1914–1918* by Maurice Baring (G Bell, 1920).

Other primary sources consulted include the papers and correspondence of Sir David Henderson, kept in the Manuscript Collections of the NLS, as well as copies of the regimental diaries of the Argyll and Sutherland Highlanders held at the Archives and Special Collections of the Mitchell Library in Glasgow.

Further sources for the story of the Hendersons and the RFC include *The Royal Flying Corps in World War One* by Ralph Barker (Robinson, 2002); *No Empty Chairs: The Short and Heroic Lives of the Young Aviators Who Fought and Died in the First World War* by Ian Mackersey (Weidenfeld & Nicholson, 2012); and *Fighter Heroes of WWI: The extraordinary story of the pioneering airmen of the Great War* by Joshua Levine (HarperCollins, 2009).

More generally, the author consulted a number of other texts about the war, including the *The Great War* by Corelli Barnett (Park Lane Press, 1979) and various entries in *The Oxford Dictionary of National Biography*.

For anyone who wants to understand the impact of the war on Scotland, and vice versa, *The Flowers of the Forest: Scotland and the First World War* by Trevor Royle (Birlinn, 2007) and *Scottish Voices from the Great War* by Derek Young (Tempus, 2006) are essential reading.

The lines of poetry by Wilfed Owen quoted in the introduction are from *Apologia pro Poemate Meo (In Defence of My Poetry)* written upon Owen's release from Craiglockhart Military Hospital, Edinburgh, in November 1917. It was taken from *Wilfred Owen: The War Poems*, edited by Jon Stallworthy, (Chatto & Windus, 1994). For more information about Wilfred Owen, visit www.wilfredowen.org.uk.

The lines of poetry by Ewart Alan Mackintosh are from *Recruiting*, a poem Mackintosh wrote in response to an army recruiting poster whose 'patriotic' drive to entice more young men to their deaths in the war angered him. It is taken from *War: The Liberator, and other pieces, with a memoir* by Ewart Alan Mackintosh (John Lane, 1918).

Any genuine omissions or errors regarding appropriate acknowledgement and usage of source material will be made good in future editions.

The author would like to thank staff (and volunteers) at the NLS, the RAF Museum archive, the Gordon Highlanders Museum, the Mitchell Library and the 'Edinburgh's War' project at Edinburgh City Libraries/Edinburgh University. Among the many individuals who informed my thinking or contributed their time, advice and/or assistance to various aspects of this book and related work I would like to thank Alison Metcalfe, Bryan Legate, Jesper Ericsson, Tess Maclean, Bert Innes, Alistair McEwen, Beverley Casebow, Andrew Simmons,

Lindsey Fraser and the editorial team at Birlinn, and illustrator extraordinaire Chris Brown. Thanks also to Faither and Uncle John.

Allan Burnett, January 2014